You Can Not Choose Your Parents

You Can Not Choose Your Parents

HELEN WOO

iUniverse, Inc.
Bloomington

You Can Not Choose Your Parents

iUniverse books may be ordered through booksellers or by contacting:

iUniverse
1663 Liberty Drive
Bloomington, IN 47403
www.iuniverse.com
1-800-Authors (1-800-288-4677)

ISBN: 978-1-4620-3153-5 (sc)
ISBN: 978-1-4620-3152-8 (dj)
ISBN: 978-1-4620-3151-1 (ebk)

Library of Congress Control Number: 2011910681

Printed in the United States of America

iUniverse rev. date: 07/07/2011

Introduction

My name is Helen Woo. I am a Chinese-American who was born in Shanghai, China. Recently I read a newspaper article about a Chinese-American college professor and the way that she chose to raise her children. Amy Chua's book is titled *Battle Hymn of the Tiger Mother*; I feel that I have so much to say about this topic. In China, many parents forced their children to do things using some of the same methods that Amy Chua used to control her children. It appears that Amy Chua is a loving mother and that she did what she thought was best for her daughters. I have no intent to criticize her; she was the stimulation for me to write this book.

As a child who was raised in a very tyrannical manner, I remember it as a painful experience. I want to write it out and tell a true story from a child's viewpoint. After all these years I still have deep feelings about my family members, but I have no wish to hurt anyone unnecessarily.

In Chinese society, receiving a high education is seemingly the only way to cast off the yolk of poverty and the only way to enter prosperity. Everyone on both sides of my family is highly educated. In my mother's family, my grandparents were the ones who held wealth and power and had absolutely authority; my grandfather's words were the final words at any time. Children's feelings and thoughts were never considered. When my mother was born, she was the fourth girl out of six children in her family (one of the older girls died at a young age) and it made my grandparents very disappointed. Just like any other Chinese family, they wanted boys to continue the family lineage. To my grandparents, my mother was just an extra child. She was treated unfairly and was looked down on by her older sisters and younger brothers because she was the youngest girl. My mother did not know how to stand up for herself, but wanted to prove to her family that she could do good things just like anyone else in order to change the opinions of her.

My mother had very high expectations of me from the first school day. She wanted me to be the best of the best in order to make her look good in other people's eyes. In order to help me get the best grades, she limited a lot of other activities, and asked me to put almost all of my time into studying. I was not allowed to play after school, nor go to any of my friends' houses. My mother would search my school bag every once in a while and throw away anything which was not study related. She could not stand it if I made mistakes, and if I did, I would get physically punished.

I was very different from my mother. I thought differently than she did, had different opinions than she did and had different tastes than she did. All of this drove my mother crazy. She could not stand it if anyone in her family had an opinion different from hers. Everything had to go her way and her way only.

Such strict supervising caused tremendous pain in my life. I did not have any freedom, was not allowed to make my own decisions, and was not allowed to do anything without my mother's or father's permission. I became so simple and naïve; I was basically a sheep that could only obey. Everything that I heard from my parents was negative, and I lacked self confidence and did not believe in myself.

I struggled and used my own way to fight back. I did a lot of things that I was not supposed to do behind my parents' back, just in order to get a little freedom and a little control of my own life.

After I immigrated to the United States in 1985, I saw the freedom that American people had which was impossible in China. I learned that the way that I was treated by my parents was called abuse, which was absolutely not a big concern in China. I also learned that American people, including children, were well protected by a much better legal system. For the first time in my life, I realized that beating people was against the law. All of this widely opened my eyes.

After many years of hard study and hard work, I used my own actions to prove to my family that I was not as bad as they thought I was. My family members and relatives thought I was stupid and would never amount to anything or that I could do anything constructive. It was beyond their expectations of me.

Now I have my own family. I live with my two daughters, Victoria and Ashley, and my husband Curt. I learned so much from my own experiences. I decided to be a stay-at-home mother and raise my daughters after they were born. I had heard of some people who were very successful in their careers but did not have good relationships with their children. I promised myself that I would not let that happen; I would not repeat my parents' mistakes.

Victoria now is in fifth grade, and Ashley is in third grade. They both study very hard in school, and have earned awards each year. They both have very outgoing personalities and many friends. Victoria is taking gymnastics classes, and Ashley is taking ballet classes; each of which was their own choice. They enjoy this very much and are doing well. I allow them to play after they finish their homework. I also allow them to go to their friends' houses and invite their friends over. I am so happy that my daughters talk to me, telling me about the things that happened in school and letting me know about the problems that they have. I am glad that they are having a happy childhood. Many years from now, these will be memories and childhood stories that they can pass on to their children.

I also would like to say to someone who was a neglected or unloved child: do not believe anyone who tells you that you are stupid. They do not know anything about you. For those ones who are unwanted by their families: do not give up. Believe and trust in God, He will look after you the way that He has promised, even though sometimes we do not understand why bad things happen. Success will be around the corner. If I could do it, than anyone could do it.

Chapter 1 – Mother's Family

My mother's father was the only son in his family. His father, my great grandfather, was a supervisor who worked for a tobacco company. When my grandfather was eighteen years old, he was sent to law school. In the late 1920s and the early 1930s, China's warlords were involved in a tangled warfare, and the government was weak. After my grandfather graduated from law school, he realized that the people who could afford to hire lawyers were the warlords. But he decided not to work for those people and became a business man instead.

My grandfather became the president of an Indonesian branch of a Chinese bank. He worked there for several years. He took his wife and two sons with him, and left three daughters behind with his mother.

When World War II broke out, my mother and her two sisters lived in Shanghai with their grandmother. Later, when the Japanese occupied Indonesia, my grandfather came back to China. He opened a manufacturing company which produced china and makeup. The makeup from his company sold very well in the market.

Back in those days, Westerners came to China for business. They opened banks, high society clubs, hotels, and other businesses. Shanghai was just like New York in the United States, and was an international city.

My grandfather had many opportunities for contact with Western businessmen for his business. In these situations, English was very necessary. He hired an English tutor to teach his children English. He himself spoke very good English, and many years later, after he had immigrated to the United States, he did not need any help with translation to communicate with people.

When his children were old enough to go to high school, they were sent to the best schools in Shanghai. The three girls were sent to the

1

American Christian Saint Mary Girl's School. The two boys were sent to the American Christian Saint John Boy's School. My mother really enjoyed the life in Saint Mary. She learned everything in English, and received training in proper manners. Because of her grades, she was allowed to take piano lessons which only the top graded girls were allowed to take. She enjoyed the social life with her friends in this school.

Everything changed when the Communist government took over. In my mother's senior year in high school, Saint Mary and Saint John were forced to close. All American employees were sent back to the United States. Saint Mary was changed to Shanghai Third High School. My mother graduated from Third High School.

My mother's oldest sister, Chen, decided to go to the United States for higher education in music. Because of her sponsorship, my entire family got to immigrate to America many years later.

My mother's other sister, O, went to college for her English major. After she graduated, she worked for the Chinese foreign ministry department to be the English teacher for the Chinese foreign minister.

My mother wanted to study pharmaceutics. She was accepted by Beijing Pharmacology College, the best pharmacology college in China. After the Chinese Communist Party took over power, they started to use their imperious policies to control people's freedom and speech. The government decided everything and Chinese people no longer had many choices in their lives. After my mother graduated from college, she was chosen to be an engineer for a pharmaceutical manufacturing company in Chongqing, an industrial city in central China.

My uncle Frank and Uncle George graduated from college later as engineers.

In the late 1950s, the Chinese Communist Party finally showed their truth colors. In order to stabilize his power, Mao Tsetung started to kill people whom he thought were against him. He also put a lot of them in jail, including college professors, businessmen, scientists, and the generals who had helped him during WWII. The political movements were one after another, spread over the whole country. High school students did not go to school. Instead, as the Red Guard, they were incited to send their teachers to jail, and put the people who they thought had enmity against the Communist Party in jail. A lot of people were killed or banished during this time.

As a businessman, my grandfather was a target of the Chinese government. Several groups of Red Guards came to my grandfather's house and sacked everything including the clothing, antiques, collections, and my grandmother's jewelry. They also ordered my grandparents to pile up their furniture and family albums in the middle of the street. They then ordered my grandparents to burn everything with all their neighbors standing around watching; this in order to embarrass them. The government confiscated my grandfather's business, cars, and all the houses he owned in Shanghai. They were forced to move into a one room apartment with a bed on one side and a dining table on the other. The bathroom and the kitchen were shared with three other families.

From 1966 to 1976, the Cultural Revolution completely destroyed Chinese traditions and Chinese culture. The Red Guards traveled all over the country. They destroyed temples, Buddha statues, and churches. The churches which had historical value were forced to close, and the books were burned; except Mao's books which were spared. It was a large loss. It only took a short time to destroy everything. It would take a longer time to recover, especially for the people who were born in the 1950s such as many of the Red Guards. They were used by Mao Tsetung; and wasted the best years of their life by being Mao's hatchet men. In this ten year period, China lost many of its best scientists, businessmen, and musicians. Anybody who was in Mao's way was sent to jail, killed, banished, or committed suicide. Mao Tsetung's government used the guarantee of a college education or a better job as methods to encourage people to keep an eye on each other. Spies were everywhere and could be someone's best friend, neighbor, or co-worker. Sometimes they wanted the husbands and wives to spy on each other.

My grandparents were suspected because Aunt Chen lived in the United States. The relationship between China and the United States was bad. The government kept a close eye on my grandparents by making them go to meetings every week. In these meetings, Mao's books and ideas were studied and discussed. There were many people around who we did not know. But we suspected them to report on all of our activities to the government.

During that time, a lot of people escaped to Hong Kong. So a fence had been built between the border of mainland China and Hong Kong to prevent this. The soldiers were ordered to kill anyone who tried to escape by this way. It was too late for my grandparents when they finally decided to go there. Aunt Chen flew to Hong Kong to meet with them, but they were unable to meet. My grandparents lost their first chance to leave the country and this caused much suffering later.

My mother, Aunt O, and Uncle George were fine because they lived in different cities far away from Shanghai and nobody knew their family background. I remember that my sister and I were not allowed to mention anything about my relatives to anyone or I would be punished. I did not even know that I had an aunt who lived in the United States until I was much older.

But Uncle Frank was sent to jail for several years. He was a member of the team who designed a submarine for the Chinese Navy. It was not because he was a criminal, but because of his family background, and because his sister lived in the United States. The Chinese government did not trust anyone like Uncle Frank working for the military.

President Nixon visited China in 1972, and Washington and Beijing started to communicate. My family saw this as an opportunity for a second chance, and we decided not to miss it. In the same year, my aunt Chen came to visit us for the first time since she left China. All the children, my sister, I, and all of our cousins were introduced to Aunt Chen for the first time. She was ready to sponsor our entire family to immigrate to the United States after she went back. By now my family was very disappointed with the Chinese government, and we did not trust their empty promises anymore. They crushed many business people like my grandfather who chose to stay and help rebuild the Chinese economy after WWII. After several years of preparation, my grandparents immigrated to the United States. Then, Aunt O and her family, Uncle Frank's family, Uncle George's family, and my own family followed. Thanks to the Lord, we immigrated to this great country.

From ancient times until present, Chinese society has never been stable enough to protect any one individual. Wealth is no guarantee for anyone. Looking back, most any group of people who were trusted by the previous emperor were killed or banished when the new dynasty was born. People always wondered how to protect themselves and their wealth so they buried their gold or silver. People did everything they could to let their children marry someone who was in a high position, hoping that could protect their children and grandchildren. But all these have no guarantee. The Chinese have a saying "the wealth is not going to last to the third generation." It became a curse that no one could avoid.

Dynasty after dynasty, year after year, people finally realized that they have to invest instead of burying their wealth. Today, people invest in the land, stocks, and business.

Like many smart people, my grandfather believed that education is the best investment. It was why he sent all his five children to the best schools to receive the best education possible. Anyone can take your money away from you, but nobody can take away your knowledge. It was proven by everything that happened to my grandparents during the Chinese Cultural Revolution. After my family immigrated to the United States, none of us spoke fluent English except Aunt O. My mother and her brothers were able to find engineering jobs because of their excellent previous experiences.

In my grandfather' house, he was always the head of the family and everyone obeyed him. The family traditions of etiquette were strictly enforced; all children were not viewed the same or treated equally. The parents were at the top, followed by Uncle Frank and Uncle George. Even though they were the youngest children, they came before their older sisters. Next was Aunt Chen, followed by Aunt O, with my mother at the very end. Everything at home followed this order. My mother was treated unfairly, and everyone looked down on her because she was the youngest daughter. But she studied hard in school; got the best grades she could, and tried to change the opinions that others had about her.

She had a strong personality, and did not like to be looked down on. She was the youngest girl in the family; and the way she was treated caused her to become frustrated. Her childhood training was to obey her parents, brothers, and sisters. She struggled against this assault on her personality, and swallowed the bitterness she felt when she did not have strong self confidence to stand up for herself. She was like a dormant volcano, looking for the right time to erupt. It exerted a tremendous negative influence in her later life.

Chapter 2 – Father's Family

Grandpa Woo, my father's father, was the oldest son of the Woo family. He was a certified chief engineer, with a salary five times higher than an engineer. He worked for an American coal mining company, and was a club member at a high society club.

Grandma Woo was the youngest daughter of her family. She was a beautiful young lady before she married, and was her parents' favorite child.

After they married, they loved each other and had a wonderful life. They had four children, two boys and two girls. My father was the second child born to them. They hired servants to work for the family. They owned an individual house and had everything a high society household needed. They attended dance parties in the club which was Grandma Woo's favorite activity. As a club member, they did not need to pay cash since everything was recorded on Grandpa Woo's club credit card which he paid at the end of each month. The family lived a better life than most Chinese.

After Mao Tsetung took over the country, Grandpa Woo, like most of the scientists that the government did not like, lost everything. He was still needed because of his educational background. The government allowed him to move into a two room apartment with a kitchen, and a full bathroom. This was the apartment in which I later spent my childhood.

My father and my mother met each other at work. They both were engineers and worked in the same department. Later, they fell in love.

In China, when two young people loved each other, they could not just announce their engagement without first asking their parents' permission. The boy had to go to the girl's house to ask permission from the girl's father.

In Chinese society, family history is important to the parents of the young couple. Marriages are only preferred to be within the same social level. My maternal grandfather nodded his approval after he checked the three generations of my father's family history.

Because of the revolutionary situation, everyone was very careful in everything they did. It was a scary time. Anybody could get in trouble for any reason, and sometimes no reason was required. Grandma Woo was not too happy about her daughter-in-law because of her family background. Just like all the trouble between the mother-in-laws and the daughter-in-laws, Grandma Woo did not treat my mother well.

Aunt Ying, who I loved very much, was my father's youngest sister. She was beautiful and had long, long hair which was braided just like Rapunzel's. Aunt Ying was a college student, and only came to visit once in a while. Every time she came, she always spoiled me by taking me out and buying me ice cream.

At this time, there were no toy stores; there was only a small toy section in certain stores. I did not have much. One day, as soon as Aunt Ying walked in the front door, I saw a beautiful doll in her arm. The doll had a beautiful smiling face, and was wearing a beautiful outfit. It was exactly the kind of doll that I always dreamed to have. I had been bothering Grandma Woo for a doll for a long time, and she had not bought one for me because it was so expensive. Aunt Ying bought me this doll with her own spending money. It was my favorite toy and I played with it every day.

Aunt Ying was my idol. I loved her from deep within my heart. I loved her kindness, her beauty, but most of all, I loved her long hair. I asked Grandpa to buy me the same long hair just like Aunt Ying's since I did not know that hair was grown, not bought.

My father's older sister, Aunt Fang, moved out from her father's home before I was born. I loved her too, but she was busy all the time, and did not come home very often. I only met her husband once in my life.

Uncle Zong, my father's youngest brother, was the spoiled one. He was ten years younger than my father; and everyone in the family treasured him. He was a handsome young man who had a lot of energy; he always dressed the best with spending money from Grandpa. He liked to boss me around. He did not have gentleness like the rest of the family members, and I did not like the way he carried me when he took me out. I was afraid of him and did not feel safe around him. One time he took me out to a place far, far away with a group of his best friends. It was Chinese New

Year's day. People shot off firecrackers right next to me. It was so loud, and he stopped me from covering my ears. It had scared me to death.

Uncle Zong's wife was a very nice lady. She was a school teacher, and had a daughter. As a child, I loved to go out with her because if she bought anything for her daughter, she must buy the same thing for my sister and me. She never let us feel that we were not included. The day before we left Shanghai, she gave my sister and me two chocolate bars for each of us. It was unheard of. Back then, chocolate bars were very expensive, and a school teacher did not make that much money. In Chongqing, the city I lived in, most of my friends never even heard of chocolate. I kept the chocolate bars for a long time just to remember her.

Just like any other spoiled person, Uncle Zong did not know to appreciate everything he had. After he married, his wife took care of their daughter, allowing him to go out and have fun with his friends every day. He did not take his father's responsibility seriously; he spent his money without leaving any for the family.

After my beloved Grandpa Woo passed away, no one gave Uncle Zong any money. He lost his support, and became very resentful. He moved in to my grandma's apartment with his wife and daughter in order to take care of Grandma, but he did not even do this job.

Grandma's teeth bothered her for her whole life; they eventually affected her health. My grandma told me that Uncle Zong ignored her one night when she had a heart problem one evening. Uncle Zong pretended like nothing happened when he heard Grandma's moaning.

When we sold everything for immigration, my father left the TV for my grandma and Uncle Zong, but he did not share it. He moved the TV into his room and Grandma had to buy another one for herself.

Chapter 3 – Early Life with Grandparents

I was born in Shanghai and was the second child in my family. My mother's first child was a boy who died during delivery. To my parents, it was more than a tragedy, because they lost a son; one who could continue the family lineage.

During this time, China was overrun with several disasters for many years. The Soviet Union stopped their support of China. They withdrew all their scientists and equipment. The Chinese government exported food to North Korea, Vietnam, and Kampuchea; countries who were their brotherhood countries. Meanwhile, a lot of Chinese people died of hunger. Most of the time their meals were corn flour buns. Every once a while, my parents treated themselves to a bowl of rice mixed with soy sauce. Meat and vegetables were not available.

In order to provide a better life for me, my parents decided to leave me with Grandpa and Grandma Woo. It was easier to get baby formula and other things that a baby needed in Shanghai.

As I grew older, I needed more and more. I wanted my grandma to play with me. I wanted her to take me to the park. It became harder for Grandma to meet my needs. When I was five, she decided to take me to a local daycare center. This daycare center provided service for the families who needed to leave their children overnight. Unfortunately, I was one of those children. Grandma Woo dropped me off every Monday morning and picked me up on every Saturday afternoon.

I was so sad because I did not understand why this happened to me. I watched everyone else go home with their parents every day, and I had to stay there with a few other kids. During the day, I stood by the window, looked out, and cried for Grandpa or Grandma to take me home.

The teachers were not friendly at all, and I did not enjoy the time when I was there. We were all treated very roughly.

During the winter I was cold at night. I could not sleep well since my feet were cold all night long. I told Grandma about it and she bought me a hot water bottle. When I returned to the school the next Monday morning, Grandma handed the hot water bottle to the teacher and asked her to put it in my blanket at night. The nanny only let me use it for the first night. After that, she let her favorite student use it. She told me that everyone had to share.

Wednesday was the day that made me happy. It was the day that my grandma came to visit in the afternoon. She brought me candy and other snacks. I was so excited. I felt that I had been loved.

My parents and my sister, Agnes, came to visit once a year when they had a business trip. But they were like strangers to me. I had no concept about "father" and "mother," and the relationship that there should be between us. In my mind, Grandpa and Grandma were the ones who raised me and they were my whole life. The people whom I called "father" and "mother" were just visitors.

I showed interest in dance since I was about six years old. From the first time I watched a ballet called "The White-Haired Girl," I could not believe my eyes that such a beautiful type of dance existed. I fell in love with ballet immediately. During that time, "The White-Haired Girl" was the only ballet in China. I would stop anything I was doing and sit by the radio every time I heard the music. I dreamed to be a ballerina one day in the future.

My parents decided to take me back when I was six years old. I was sent to live with Aunt O, who lived in Wuhan, a city between Shanghai and Chongqing, for a short time, waiting for somebody to pick me up.

One day, I was so surprised to see Uncle Zong who came to take me back to Shanghai. My grandpa missed me so much, and cried out in his dreams at night. He could not stand the time without me. So I was taken back to live with my grandparents for another half year.

Chapter 4 – Early Life with Parents

My life with my beloved Grandpa and Grandma came to an end at the age of six and a half. A friend of my parents' picked me up, and I was on another journey back to Chongqing. I had to face a new situation, a new life, and a family of my own who were but strangers to me since I was born.

I did not like this family. My parents and Agnes were nice to me, but they were strangers to me. I did not know anybody, and I had a hard time communicating with anyone because I did not speak the local dialect. Most of the words were pronounced completely differently from the ones that I knew. I did not know the games that the neighbor kids played; they made fun of me because of the way I talked. I felt so lonely and could not stop thinking about my grandpa and grandma. My sister was four years old. She and I got along well and I enjoyed playing with her. I shared the toys that I brought with me and shared the toys that she already had.

I also had a hard time in kindergarten understanding and communicating with other kids. I remember Agnes cried and screamed every morning and did not want to go. I felt the same way. Actually, from the very beginning, I never felt comfortable to talk to my parents, either. I learned to hide my feelings. Every time when Agnes cried and screamed, my mother would say to her "go to school today, but tomorrow you do not have to go," in order to comfort her. She promised us this many time, but we never got to stay at home. So I started to question her promises.

One day, after my mother dropped us off at school, I convinced Agnes to go back home with me, because mother had promised us that that day we did not have to go to school. We did this. The problem was the house key. We did not have a key, and we were afraid to meet people that my parents worked with who might tell on us. The company that my parents worked for was right next to the apartment where the employees lived; there was only a small empty field between the two buildings. My sister and I hid in the apartment building next to ours for several hours, behind the gates. Finally, a man noticed that we were the kids next door, and notified the security guard. My father made himself very clear that I would get a spanking if it happened again.

As time passed by, their true personalities started to show. Slowly, I found out that they both were simmering volcanoes. They had no patience with me, and no loving heart towards me. They also wanted me to completely obey them, or I would be physically punished. All of this was directed towards me, and not at my sister.

In kindergarten, I was a slow eater; I was almost always one of the last ones who finished lunch. The teacher would scream at me to finish, and tell on me to my parents. I did not understand why this happened to me. I was never hungry, and all of us kids had to finish two bowls of rice no matter what. I could not swallow the food under such pressure. No one comforted me, or talked to me, or tried to find a solution for me. I just had to obey.

One day, things got worse. It was time to go home after lunch. The kids left the cafeteria one after one until just one boy and I were left sitting there because we had not finished lunch. The teacher told us that we could not go until we finished the last piece of rice. My father was waiting outside. As usual, I could not swallow the food no matter how hard I tried, even though I knew what kind of punishment was waiting for me. As soon as I walked out the door, I saw my father's long face. He did not say anything for several minutes, and then the volcano erupted. My father slapped me and kicked me on my bottom. I fell onto the ground in front of all the other kids and their parents. I was so embarrassed. After my mother found out what had happened, she turned into an angry lion. She took out a chopstick and stuck it into my mouth and threatened to push down the food for me. I was scared to death.

I wet the bed almost every night. I could not help it. I slept so deeply and hardly woke up. My parents did not know what to do with me, so they beat me every time it happened. They blamed me for not going to the bathroom earlier and said that I was lazy. They locked me in the bathroom at midnight, and would not let me sleep. I did not mean to do it. I did not want to wet the bed, but I could not help it. I stopped drinking water after seven o'clock in the evening. I tried not to fall asleep, so that I could go to bathroom if I needed. I did everything a little kid could think of to stop wetting the bed. I had nightmares almost every night. In the dreams, I was looking for the bathroom everywhere, but I could not find it. Sometimes, I found the bathroom; I was afraid to go, because I was not sure if it was real life or if it was just a dream. When I woke up the next day, the bed was wet. It happened to me over and over again for almost one year. Meanwhile, neither my father nor my mother tried to wake me up at midnight to let me use the bathroom, nor did they take me to a hospital. They did nothing but beat me.

The six and one half years that I lived with my grandpa and grandma caused a deep gap between my parents and me. They realized that I was not raised the way that they wanted me to be raised. The way I talked or the way I did things reminded my mother about her in-laws who did not treat her nice. She was bitter and took her frustration out on me every time I did something wrong.

My parents started to treat me differently than Agnes. They yelled at me if there was an argument between Agnes and me, without finding out what was really going on. It did not matter what we got, they let Agnes choose first. Agnes always got bigger and better things than I did. I was not allowed to complain.

One night after dinner, we had oranges for dessert. My father split the oranges into several pieces. As usual, Agnes got the biggest pieces. I swapped one of my small pieces for a big piece from her when I thought that no one was paying attention, but my father saw it. He thought about it, then took another orange out and gave to her.

We lived on the third floor in a two room apartment. There were ten families, including us, who lived on the same floor. Our apartment was really more like two one-room apartments, since the hallway separating the two rooms was actually a common hallway used by all families for cooking. People put their stoves, garbage cans, and their coal containers in the hallway. One room was the bedroom with all the good furniture. It was decorated beautifully, was very comfortable, and was where my parents and Agnes slept. The room on the other side of the hallway was mainly for dining, with the things for cleaning and washing on one side and a small bed on the other side. This was the place where I slept every night. This was the way that my parents kept me separated from them for many years. I did not mind at all for I had a private place for myself every night, where I could look out the window, or read, or daydream. I absolutely loved it.

In my mind, this was my room and the other room was their room. I did not like to go into their room unless it was necessary.

My parents never played with Agnes and me from the time that we were young. They thought it was ridiculous for parents to play with their children, and thought that children should play with children. They never read for us. They did not tell us stories until we were older. My parents were very different from other kids' parents. They were very serious and were too strict for me.

Chapter 5 – Early Difficulties

It was time to go to elementary school when I was seven years old. My mother had very high expectations for me from the first day. She took me out to buy everything that I needed for school. She told me to study as hard as I could and to get the best grades that I could to honor the family. Of cause, she did not forget to warn me that I would be physically punished if I did not meet these expectations.

My father thought that I was old enough to do some house work. Every evening after dinner, I washed everyone's handkerchiefs and swept the floor.

A Chinese students' life is one of the hardest in the world. We had so much homework to do from the beginning of first grade. After school, I had to write Chinese characters repeatedly, many characters per line for several pages. But I enjoyed doing it; it was new to me. If I did well, it would make my mother proud, and make me happy. I learned simple adding and subtracting in math class, and learned new songs in music class. All of this was fine until I got older.

After I went into the second grade, I had some problems in math class. On the returned homework, I received several red "Xs", meaning it was the wrong answer. My mother could not stand it. She could put up with one or two red "Xs", but definitely not several red "Xs." She turned into an angry lion when she was angry and slapped me. Sometimes I came home with some of my friends, but it did not stop my mother from slapping me in front of them.

In Chinese society, a child is the parents' personal property, just like anything else that they own. They can treat their children any way they want to treat them. Parents are never considered to be wrong and anything they do is for their children's own good. The society never blames parents for bruises from abuse. This tradition is passed on from generation to generation. Chinese parents strongly believe that with enough beatings, a child can be trained to be a dutiful child. So when a child is beaten, nobody says anything about it, because it is not against any of their laws. This way usually is used on boys, not on girls, and has been used by many Chinese parents. They think it is a family issue and that nobody has the right to judge them. Many years after I grew up, I realized the reason that my parents treated me this way was because they wanted to raise me as a boy in order to compensate them for the earlier loss of their son.

They had no problem to embarrass me in front of my friends, in a public place like school, or on the street. They thought it could stimulate me, change my behavior, or make me become a better person. In order to help me get the best grades that I could get, they would not let me play with my friends after school. They wanted me to put all of my time into studying. I had to be home on time. If I was late, I had to report to them where I was. I had to do homework as soon as I got home, and continually did extra homework after dinner until bed time. As a child, I found all kinds of excuses to go out with my friends. I learned to lie to my parents, and also learned ways to avoid the punishment for that. Many times, I lied that I had some kind of school activity, so that I could go to school and play. I lied that I needed pencils or notebooks, so I could go to the store. I would look around, watch the blue sky, and breathe the fresh air. This was the only time that I could relax. After a while, I could lie so well that many times my parents believed me. It got to the point where any excuse could pop out my mouth without me having time to even think about it.

My parents hated when I lied to them. They wanted me to be an honest person, and listed all the bad things that could happen to me if I lied. They punished me and took my things away from me, or did not allow me to do certain things. But it did not get better. I still lied in order to get my freedom.

One night after dinner, when I asked my father if he could let me go to school to take the quiz that the teacher required, he questioned me.

"Are you sure you have a quiz this evening, or do you just want to play?" he asked me.

"Yes, you can ask any of my friends if you want to," I said to him.

"All right. But come home as soon as possible. Like I told you many times before, you need to study."

My father went to school to check on me later that evening. He found out that I lied again. Two hours later, when I got home, he questioned me.

"How did the quiz go?"

"It went OK."

"I don't think so. I think you went somewhere else."

"I did not, really."

"I went to your school. I didn't see any lights on in any of the buildings. All the school buildings were empty," my father said.

"I am sorry; I went to a friend's house. But she asked me to." I tried to blame my friend, hoping that my father would not punish me too hard.

That night, I got beaten up.

When my parents physically punished me, they used a bamboo stick to hit my bottom, my legs, and my arms. My mother also liked to slap me on my face. The blood was all over my lips and arms. My lips would be swollen afterwards. During the summer, everyone could see the bruises on my arms, and legs.

"I will beat you so hard, that you will never forget it for the rest of your life," my father would say to me when he was angry. This was the way that my parents used to teach me in my childhood. My parents strongly believed it was the only way to teach. But they never taught my sister this way, only me.

Studying was the biggest thing in my life. It took up most of the time during the day if there was no school. My parents worked in the building next to our apartment building. My room faced the window of a conference room in that building, which just happened to be at the same level with our apartment. So from across the empty field, my parents could spy on me at any time. There was a gap between the curtains and the bottom of the window. From this gap, my parents could see what was on my desk. I was so amazed at how good my parents' eyesight was. My father came home at different times during the day, just to check on me.

My mother gave me ten minutes to walk home after school. If I was late, I had to have a good explanation for it. Every Saturday afternoon, before the kids went home from school, we had to clean the classroom. Wiping the floor, washing the desks and chairs, and washing the blackboard were all tasks for us to do. Since we were kids, we enjoyed playing while we were cleaning. It took a little longer time than on the week days. I enjoyed it so much because it was my opportunity to play with my friends.

One Saturday, my mother had a bad day, so she was in a bad mood. After I got home, she wanted to know why I was late.

"I was cleaning," I answered.

"Why did it take so long? Are you sure that you did not go somewhere else?"

"No, mother. You can ask my friends or the teacher, if you want."

"It should not take such a long time to clean. Let me see, five minutes is enough to wipe the floor, ten minutes is enough to wash the desks and chairs, another five minutes is enough to wash the blackboard. You are thirty minutes late. You better tell me where you have been."

I did not know what to say to her. This was my mother. She did not see this from a child's point of view, and instead judged me from an adult's point of view.

I was hoping that my parents would let me go out just like my friends could. They could go out if they finished their homework and they did not have to do any extra homework. Every time when we had a plan, I was the only one who could not attend, because my parents would not allow it. After this happened many times, I was not invited any more. It broke my heart.

I felt like a bird which was locked in a cage without any freedom. I liked to watch the sky; the blue sky and the white clouds always made me happy. I dreamed that there would be a day in the future when I could fly somewhere far, far away, somewhere where nobody would yell at me or beat me. I felt that the time passed by so slowly as I was waiting for the day when I would grow up, make my own decisions, and have my freedom.

I loved reading; I could read for hours and hours. The stories took my mind away so that I forgot the unhappy things that were happening to me. Every night after my father, my mother, and my sister went into their bedroom; I turned on the light, and read for several hours. Sometimes, when my mother got up to use the bathroom, she found that the light in my room was still on. She was angry, and I was slapped. But it did not stop me from reading after bed time.

Dancing was another thing that made me very, very happy. I taught myself by watching other people dance. I could dance at any time, in any empty room.

One summer afternoon, my grandma took me out and we passed by a store. In the store window, I saw a pair of pink ballet pointed shoes. I stood there for a long time, staring at the most beautiful shoes in the world, and imagined that I was dancing with these shoes on my feet. I begged Grandma to buy me the shoes, but she did not because they were too expensive. After we went home, Grandma told my father about it.

"You want those shoes? What are you going to do with them? Wear them to school to show off?"

I had nothing to say to him. I did not know what to say to him.

Every holiday, I was selected to be the dancer for the celebration activities in the school. I was the best dancer. I had a very good memory for every dance movement; I was born for dancing. I always got the best complements from people.

Unfortunately, there was no dance school available. The only one that I knew of was in Shanghai. Every time my parents took my sister and me to the zoo, the bus passed by the Shanghai Ballet School and my eyes filled with tears. This was the school to which I dreamed to go. The only one that I felt comfortable to talk to about this was my grandma, but she thought ballet was too hard to learn. My parents just wanted me to study and go to college in the future. College education was the only thing on their mind. They wanted me to follow their advice and be who they wanted me to be. They did not consider my interests or listen to me when I tried to voice them. I felt that my parents did not understand me, because they never seriously talked to me in order to find out where my interests were. I did not know how to find a way to let my parents know what I wanted to do. Everybody knew that I loved to dance, and that I danced well; I could not find anyone who could persuade my parents to let me go to ballet school. I was so disappointed, and there was nothing I could do about it.

My aunt Fang had left an accordion at our apartment. My mother decided to teach me to play it. She taught me herself from her memories of piano lessons from when she was a teenager. I was the wrong person to learn any instrument. I could not read the music book, and had to stare at the key board when I played, or I would make mistakes. The apartment walls were very thin so that anybody could hear when I practiced; there was no privacy at all. I had to practice two hours every day. If one day I did not practice, my neighbor would ask me why.

After I learned to play, I was selected to be the one who played the music for the dancers in the school celebration activities. I was the best dancer in the school, but I could not dance. I only could play the music for other kids and watch them dance.

Before we immigrated to the United States, my mother decided to sell the accordion, and I was so happy. I have not played the accordion to this day.

Chapter 6 – Strict Supervision

I studied most lessons very well in school. Chinese language, foreign language, and science were no problem for me. But math was always a problem. I had to spend so much time to study it. The grades from my math homework were not good; I always had many problems wrong. It made my mother very angry, and she made me do extra math homework. She and my father spent a lot of time sitting next to me to help me, but it was not good help. My parents did not have patience, and if I did not figure out how to do the math problem quickly, my mother would slap me and my father would tell me that his hand was getting very itchy.

This meant that he just about to beat me. Usually under such pressure, I would work even slower. I was scared to death, could not think straight, and ended up getting a spanking. Many times I did math homework until three o'clock in the morning. I hated studying math and eventually I stopped asking my parents any questions about it.

My parents' expectations were too high for me; they wanted me to be the best of the best. They compared me with other kids and even with my sister. In their mind, I was never good enough and someone else was always better. In order to help me be a better person, they always pointed out the negative side of me. They had an eagle eye for the things that I did not do well enough, and were silent for the things that I did well. To them, the things that I did well were no big deal since anyone could do it. Because what I heard from my parents was always negative, I did not have self confidence, nor did I believe that I could do things well.

If I had any problem or arguments with other kids, my parents were almost always on the other people's side. To them, other people were honest and right. If there was a liar, then it must be their own daughter.

"Did you do it?" they asked me.

"No, it was not me, Father."

They slapped me, and asked again, "Did you do it?"

"No, I did not do it. It was not me."

They slapped me again and again, until I said, "Yes, I did it. I am sorry."

I surrendered under my parents' might.

I absolutely hated the parent-teacher conferences. It was the time that the teacher would tell on the students. The teachers only told the parents about the negative side of the students. Some times, my mother would go to school and talk to the teacher to find out how I was doing in school. Or she would talk to the kids who were in the same classroom with me. It gave the kids who did not like me a chance to tell on me.

All the kids knew that I would get in trouble if I did not go home on time after school, and they knew that I was not allowed to play after school. Some times, they could not find enough kids to play a game, and they would ask me to play. Deep in my heart, I would have loved to, but I knew that I could not. Most of the kids were very nice to me and felt sorry for me. But there was one particular girl who was the only daughter in her family and was spoiled. She was mean to me all the time. She liked to pick on me, boss me around, or tell on me. She knew the situation that I faced and loved to take advantage of me. She asked me to lie to my parents and play with her. Either way I would get in trouble. I never won.

Many times I skipped a class that I thought was not important, such as music class. I would go to the park with some of the kids from the same classroom. We would have our fun and come back two hours later, and nobody found out that we were missing. It was great. I enjoyed doing it. If my parents found out and beat me, it was no big deal. The important thing was that I had fun, so I did not mind to take a risk.

The way that we were taught in the school was very strict. I did well in other classes like Chinese language, foreign language, history, geography, and politics. The politics class was required in the middle school and the high school, by the government, in order to brainwash us. I had such a good memory for what I read, that I could almost remember the whole book.

Chinese students are not allowed to challenge the teachers or the experts. It was the way that we were taught. We had to learn everything that was given to us. The things to learn were put in the text books for us by these experts. There was only one correct answer which was the one provided. All we students needed to do were remember the materials, and we would get good grades. This way of learning did not challenge a student's imagination or help a student's creative skills.

Seemingly everyone knows that Chinese students do very well in math or spelling competitions, and that they get good grades in elementary school, middle school, high school, and even in college. Only those who get the best grades have a chance to go to the best schools. Only those who graduate from the best schools, have a chance to go to the best colleges. And only those who graduate from the best colleges have a chance to get good job opportunities.

Chinese students become slaves to their grades and victims of this education system. Getting the best grades becomes the only thing in their lives and everything else is put off to the side.

This is a big defect in the Chinese education system. No Chinese scientists with a Chinese college education have won a scientific Nobel Prize yet; most Chinese who have won a Nobel Prize were educated in the West.

My mother wanted me to obey her for anything, and everything had to go her way. But I thought so differently from her. We had different tastes, different opinions, and different ideas. It drove her crazy. If I did not read her mind, she would be very angry.

I always wished that I could have long hair just like my aunt Ying's, but my mother kept my hair short, because she did not like a long hair style. She decided what was for dinner, how I dressed myself, where to go or what to do, and how to do it. If there was any thing that did not go her way, or did not meet her expectations, she would be angry.

"Mother, which coat shall I wear tomorrow?"

"Why can't you decide? Do you have a brain? Can you think? Why do you ask me for every little thing like this? I am tired of it."

"OK mother, how about the gray one?"

"No, wear the green one."

Each year, my sister and I were required to write a letter to our grandparents. It was a painful time for me. My mother was never satisfied with the letter that I wrote. Each time she would read it after I finished. If she did not like the way I wrote it, I had to rewrite the letter again and again until she was satisfied. When she was finally satisfied, the letter was no longer mine; it was the way that my mother wanted it to be.

Slowly, I became a sheep. I could not read her mind. I asked her what to do, and how to do it, in order to have a peaceful day. I did not know how to make my own decisions; I only obeyed because it was all I knew. I did not have any self confidence, and was afraid to do anything without my parents' approval. I did not know how to talk properly in public. The more I made mistakes, the fewer chances that my mother gave me, because she did not want to be embarrassed.

One day, my father took out the back of a clock to show my sister and me how a clock works. I was very interested in this. The next day when my parents were at work, I invited a neighbor boy into my apartment and took out the back of the clock. We stared at the parts inside the clock and watched them move. At this moment, my father appeared at the front door. He was very angry when he saw what was going on.

"I will beat you to death if that clock stops working," he yelled at me.

I lost interest in learning anything.

Just like any child, I made mistakes and said wrong things, too. In order to avoid being embarrassed in public, my mother had me keep quiet. She would not let me handle things myself, so I lost the opportunity to learn from my mistakes. The Chinese have a saying that "mistakes are the mother of success." My mother did not understand it and had too high expectations of me. She wanted me to be the best so that it would make her look good in other people's eyes. The most important thing was to prove to her parents, sisters, and brothers that she could do good things; she wanted them to change their opinions about her.

My mother thought that her way was the best way, and that she was doing all these things for me for my own good. She thought I was too young to know what was good for me in my future. She always said to me that I could avoid a lot of mistakes in my life if I listened to her advice.

Under this strict supervising, I became so naive and simple, and only knew how to obey. Somebody had to tell me what to do, or I would get lost.

On the other hand, my mother was tired of being asked about every single little thing. She complained to other relatives in the family that I was stupid, that I could not make my mind, and that I had to be told what to do. It seemed to me that the person she wanted me to be was dependant on the situation that she was in.

She did not just treat me this way; she also treated my father badly. Playing checkers was my father's hobby. He played it very well and spent a lot of time playing with his friends. My mother did not like that; she argued with my father and asked him not to play too much. But my father did not listen. It was the main reason for arguments between them. One day my mother found out that my father played checkers at his friend's apartment. She went there and pushed the set onto the ground. My father usually never told me anything, but one time he said to me "Your mother wanted everyone to obey her, and I would not."

They argued more and more, until they argued almost every day. I was so afraid when they argued that my mother would later take her anger out on me. This had happened many times before.

We had a school meeting one day. It usually started at 7:30 a.m. But for some reason, this time the teacher announced the meeting would start at 7:00 a.m. My mother did not believe me when I told her about it.

"The meeting always starts at 7:30 a.m. Why does it start at 7:00 a.m. today?" she asked.

"I do not know."

"You're lying to me. You're trying to go to school early so you can play. Isn't that it?"

"No. I did not lie to you. But the teacher did not explain the reason," I said to her.

"I do not believe you. You are not going to school today until you tell me the truth."

I repeated my answer again and again. She started to get angry because I did not give her the answer that she wanted. She lost patience and started slapping me. Later in the day, she asked me to go to school and find out the real reason why the meeting was early. My teacher explained to me because it was going to rain, and the meeting was taking place outside.

"I am not happy. I am still going to slap you. Why do not you explain to me earlier?" my mother said to me.

Sometimes there was no trouble for several days. But it was not a good sign to me. If there were three days of peace, then I knew there would be huge trouble on the fourth day. My mother's frustration would erupt on that day; I dreaded when that day came. I much preferred to have small troubles daily.

I heard a saying that "if the mother is not happy, then nobody is happy." It was so true. Because of my mother's personality, we had so much unhappiness in our family. When she angry with me, my father never stood up and said anything for me; he thought that I was the trouble maker. He did not know how to handle situations when his wife was angry, and blamed me for her anger.

"We have so much unhappiness because of you. I wish I did not have you as my daughter. I wish I could kick you out of this family," he said to me sometimes.

"Why always you? Why do you always cause trouble? Why can't you make your mother happy?" he shouted at me at other times.

And most crushing of all; "We do not love you. This is the way it is. Do not think that you are a big deal to us just because you are our daughter. We will be fine without you. We still have your sister."

My father let my mother take out all her frustration on me. He thought if he let my mother erupt, that everything would be peaceful after that. But things did not work that way. Several times after my mother spanked me too hard, she scared my sister, Agnes. Agnes held my mother's arm and cried out "Please stop, mother. Do not spank her any more."

"Get lost. Get out. Go anywhere. Just don't stand in front of me. I am so sick of looking at your face," my mother would scream at me. So I had to stand in the hallway. When she came out for cooking, she would then tell me to "Get out, go somewhere far, far away. I never want to see you again."

I only could stand on the balcony for hours. The balcony was located between the stairs, which was the place where people would go in and out of their apartments. When this happened, everyone knew that I was in trouble again. I was so embarrassed and could only stare at the ground to avoid people's strange looks.

I did not know when this kind of life would come to an end. I was waiting for the day when I would be grown up and people would treat me better. I was too young to understand that the day I was waiting for would never come unless I fought for it.

I loved when we had visitors; they were like benefactors to me. My parents would put their best masks on only when someone came to visit. I had figured this out when I was in the second grade. I liked to invite my friends home in order to avoid possible punishment. The visitors could be my parents' friends, or neighbors, or just the kids from next door. They smiled, and talked, and laughed with my parents. This would be the only time that they were nice to me.

I was especially happy when my mother told me that Aunt Ying and her family were going to stop by and live with us for several days. It was a very special time for me. I knew I would have peace for several days. I enjoyed every moment of this visit.

My parents had several best friends. I loved them very much. My mother was always happy when they came to visit. They joked, and talked about the things that happened at work. We had dinner together sometimes, and I enjoyed their company.

One time my mother's parents visited us for two weeks. It was the biggest thing for my mother. She prepared everything, re-arranged the furniture, and made sure everything was perfect in order to please her parents. During these two weeks, she did not check my homework, and I did not have to do any extra homework. She was very nice to me. We took my grandparents to the parks, took them out for dinner, had a picnic, and took family pictures. I enjoyed this peaceful time so much. Only in this kind of situation did I feel that I was one of the family members.

The other visitors that I loved very much were my mother's aunt and her daughter. For this visit, they brought us snacks from Shanghai. They told us stories about visiting Uncle Frank and Uncle George. Everybody laughed and had a good time. They asked my father if they could take me with them to a famous ancient temple which was built a thousand years ago. My father said yes. I was so excited and I felt that I was so special. Usually only Agnes got this kind of opportunity.

It was a three day trip. On the first day, we took a five hour bus ride, and arrived at the temple in the afternoon. For the next two days, we visited different parts of this temple. We talked to the people who were in the same tourist group as we were, and had dinner together. We saw the biggest laying Buddha statue in the world, and another Buddha statue that had a thousand arms, with each hand holding a different musical instrument. It was amazing. We also saw a lot of the Buddha statues that were broken by the Red Guards during the Cultural Revolution. I went to the top of a tower which was built one thousand years ago. I enjoyed the time without my parents and my sister around me so much and I never forgot this special trip.

Chapter 7 – Summer Breaks and Travel

I had to do more house work as I got older. I washed the dishes, took out the garbage, mopped the floor, washed my own clothes, and washed my own bed sheets. By the time I was in high school, I went grocery shopping every morning. Back in those days, we did not have a refrigerator. We had to buy meat and vegetables every day. My job was to buy the vegetables, wash them and put them on the side for dinner. There was no heat in the winter, no air conditioning in the summer. The temperature inside the house was the same as the temperature outside. I washed everything in cold water, and in winter, my fingers would be ice cold.

In the summer, I mopped the bamboo bed sheets every day for everyone which kept us cool at night. I went to the ice company and waited for two or three hours in the hot afternoon sun to buy ice cubes. Many times my mother cooked green bean soup for desert. We put sugar and ice cubes in the soup, and I just loved it.

During the summer break, the weather was too hot to study, so I had a lot of time to play.

Chongqing was a city which was located on the top of a mountain. The city was split into two parts; half of the city was on top of the mountain and was the commercial center. The other half was at the bottom of the mountain. The city was surrounded by two big rivers. Every year from May to September, the weather was hot and humid. The temperature could get to 100° F in June, July and August. Since we did not have air conditioning, the company that my parents worked for gave everyone a two hour lunch break to avoid the hottest time of the day.

After May, we could not cook any more due to the heat. We bought lunch and dinner from the cafeteria. In the afternoon, Agnes and I would take a long nap.

During the evening, the flying ants would swarm all over the sky, chased by bats. They were not harmful, and did they destroy anything. I would put a container of water under the light, and soon it would fill up with ants. We would not feel any cool air until after mid-night. People liked to sit together and talk after dark, each with their own fan in hand. It was impossible to do homework in these kinds of weather conditions. I was happy even if I had a lot of house work to do during the day. I enjoyed watching the summer sky after dark; the stars were so beautiful. I was interested in astronomy and read the few astronomy books that I could find over and over again. Life was happy and peaceful during the summer.

Every year my parents took a business trip to Shanghai. They took Agnes and me out of school if it was not during the summer break. We traveled by train or by ship. If we took the train, it would take three days and two nights for a one way trip. If we took a ship, it would take five days to go to Shanghai, and would take eight days to come back. This was because Chongqing was on the upper reaches of the Yangtze River, and Shanghai was on the lower reaches. I had many reasons to love these trips. I did not have to do any homework. I could enjoy the beautiful countryside view, watch my parents talk to their co-workers, listen to their jokes, or their work discussions. My parents were extremely nice to me during these trips. My mother would prepare some special snacks for Agnes and me. I was allowed to sleep in every morning. The train or ship would stop at some of the big cities over night and we could visit those cities when they did stop. I enjoyed the vibrations of the ship or the train when I would go to sleep at night since it helped me sleep better. Everybody was in a good mood.

During these trips, I could visit my beloved Grandpa and Grandma after we got to Shanghai. Agnes and I took turns to live with both grandparents for several days. I begged my grandma Woo to talk to my father to let me stay with them and let Agnes stay with my mother's parents. My father agreed.

I felt that I had my childhood life all over again. I slept with my grandma in her bed at night, and would tell her everything about myself and how much I missed her. My grandma took me out to my favorite parks or for shopping. She bought me ice cream that was only available in Shanghai. We stopped by local restaurants for lunch and my grandma bought snacks just for me. I was the only one. It meant that I did not have to let my sister chose first, or share with her, or let her take the biggest ones for herself and leave me the ones that she did not want. I felt so special and loved.

My beloved Grandpa Woo passed away in 1976, and I became even closer to my grandma after that. She took me to visit her sister, the other one who loved me very much since I was a little child. My grandma's sister was a lady who lived in the village in her whole life and did not have much. But every time when she came to visit, she always brought me an ice cream bar. She was so kind to me and loved me more than she loved her own grandchildren. My grandma and her sister were the two most important people in my life. Even today I still love older people. I always feel comfortable to talk to them and I love their smiles. They remind me about my grandma and her sister.

Before we would leave Shanghai, I would ask Grandma to give me one of her personal things; it could be anything. It could be a small box, a handkerchief, or a coin purse. I would hide it in a secret place; it was mine. When I looked at it, it was just like looking at my grandma. It gave me comfort when I had a bad day. I would hold it in my hand when I cried or would talk to it when I felt sad.

Shanghai was an international city, so modern, so beautiful, and so filled with energy. People dressed much better here than anywhere else in the country. My mother loved to shop there. She bought many things every time we went there. I remember that she always took Agnes and me to the shoe store, or to the fabric store. Those stores were such boring places to us. We kids liked to go to the food store; this was a big, three floor department store. It was filled with the smell of ice cream as soon as we walked in. Vanilla ice cream with chocolate coating, other flavors of ice cream, cakes with cream on top, or dried plums and all other kinds of candy; all of these things were only available to us here in Shanghai. My parents bought many snacks to take back to Chongqing. They gave candy to their co-workers as a gift. Then they locked the rest in a cabinet. Only during certain times of the day would my father give Agnes and me some. But it was not enough for us since they were so delicious. He would give us more if Agnes begged. But I never begged no matter how much I wanted the candy. I never felt comfortable to tell my parents about my true feelings and my true thoughts. And they never asked, or talked to me like other kids' parents did.

When I was bored, I would look around the room, and try to find something interesting to do. I wished I could be like any of my friends who had the freedom to go out, and had their own spending money to buy anything they wanted. I tried to figure out how to reach to the snacks in the cabinet.

In the morning before my father went to work, he would double check the cabinet and make sure it was locked. But there were several times that he forgot to take the keys out before heading to work. It would take him about five minutes to return if he remembered that he forgot about his keys. After I was sure that he arrived at his office, which I could verify by spying on him from the gap at the bottom of the window, I would take out pieces of chocolate, dried plums, or some candy. I would make sure that I only took a little from each bottle and hide them. After that, I would shake the bottle, and put it down very carefully, making sure it was not too obvious that something was missing. If my father returned for the keys, I would have to let him in, and I would make sure that he could see me from outside the apartment as I walked to the front door from my desk. I did not want him to see me anywhere near the cabinet. In this way, my father would not question me or be suspicious about me. It happened several times and my father never found out.

When we went on field trips, everyone was well prepared. The kids brought candy, bread, dried plums, and other snacks. Almost everyone had some spending money. I only had two flour buns, split in half with some scrambled eggs in the middle, and very little candy. My father gave me some money, but he would not let me spend it freely.

"Save the money for an emergency only or you have to give it back. I will check later," he would say to me.

We kids liked to look for partners in order to share each other's food and snacks. We liked to look for someone who had many different kinds of food and snacks to be our partners. From this, we could tell who was treated well by their parents and who had a better family situation. It meant more than just sharing food. As one of the kid who did not have much to share, I only could find some kids who nobody else wanted as a partner.

At lunch time, the kids would sit together in their own groups. They took out their food and would eat and laugh. I struggled, watching them freely buying anything that they wanted. As a child who was never allowed to do anything without her parents' permission, I was lost. I did not know what to do when my parents were not around. Was this the emergency situation that my father was talking about, since everyone was buying something? Did I have the right to buy anything, just like everyone else? There were some snacks in the store that I wanted. What would I do if I spent the money and it was not the emergency that my father talked about? I finally decided to buy the snacks. During the rest of the trip, I spent a lot of time preparing my excuses to explain to my father why I spent the money.

I learned how to tell from my parents' body language what kind of mood that they were in. I could tell very well by watching my mother's face. It helped me to take some early actions to avoid trouble that I might get later.

One day, my mother had a long face almost all day. From my experience, I knew that we were not going to have a peaceful evening, during which she planned to have an English lesson for Agnes and me. I invited a friend of my mother's to come to our apartment after dinner. I told him that my mother needed his help to fix a clock which she had mentioned several times before. Agnes and I did not have an English lesson that evening.

After I started high school, my grades dropped. Math was more and more difficult for me to understand. I also had problems with physics and chemistry, and I stopped turning to my parents for help. At school, the teacher offered the evening classes for the students who needed help. I signed up, but it was for other reasons.

After Mao Tsetung died, the Chinese people started to break down the invisible walls that were around them. They started reaching out to the West, especially to the United States and Europe. On the street, we could see Western tourists. On the radio, we could hear Beethoven's and Mozart's symphonies. On TV, we could enjoy the Western ballets like Swan Lake, La Sylphide, and others. I realized that there were many beautiful ballets in the world. I only watched the Western ballets a few times, but it was enough. It opened my eyes.

One of my best friends had a pair of pointed ballet shoes. I went to her house every evening. We would go to our favorite place, and then put on the pointed shoes and dance and dance. They hurt my feet very badly because they did not fit. But I did not mind at all; I was in my own imagination, and I was dancing on the stage. But one day, my father found out that I was not going to school for studying. I told him the truth and everything was over.

My test grades started to fall. The math, physics, and chemistry tests were below 60%. I got beaten up every time it happened. Sometimes my mother did not have enough energy to beat me, so she let me wait until my father got home in the evening. Then my father would beat me.

I thought about committing suicide. I thought about escaping. One morning I put a few things into a package, took all the spending money that I had which had been given to me by my father, and left home. I wanted to go to Shanghai. I wanted to live with my grandma since she was the one who loved me and was the one I could depend on. I did not know how to do it, and I did not know if I had enough money or not. I just knew that I had to buy a train ticket. I sat in the waiting room at the train station for one day and one night by myself. Then I went to my friend's house to ask for help. After my friend and her mother heard my story, they showed their sympathy by letting me stay with them for a couple of days. During these two days, I saw how much my friend's mother loved her daughter and the happy family life they had. My friend did not need to watch her mother's face all the time. She did not need to lie to her mother. She did not need to steal snacks. Everyone was talking and laughing around the dining table at dinner time. If any of them had wanted to adopt me, I would not say anything, and would never have left.

Two days later, my friend's mother thought I should go home. She said to me that every mother would worry if her daughter was missing. She could not understand how I felt; she could not understand the situation that I lived in. She thought it was a regular mother and daughter argument. She sent her daughter to my home to tell my parents that I was at her house and that I was fine. The next day, my friend walked me home. In order to comfort me, she promised that she would stop my parents if they tried to beat me.

From the way that my neighbors watched me, I could tell that everyone knew I was missing for two days. It was a big thing. It was a big step for me. It was unheard of in China.

But things did not get that much better after all this. I was a teenager now. I still did the things that I was not supposed to do. In doing this, I felt that I had a little freedom and that I had a little bit of control of my life. Of course, I did all this behind my parents' back. I started to change the grades on my test since we were graded as 100, 90, 80, 70 instead of A, B, C, D. It was easy. I could make my grades look better in front of my parents and they would leave me alone for a while. They never found out the truth.

Agnes and I were old enough to stay home by ourselves. My parents stopped taking us for their business trips. She was spoiled and very self-centered. Since she was young, she never had to do any house work. She was allowed to do anything she wanted, in any way that she wanted. She had all the freedom that I was never allowed to have. When she played games with me, I had to let her win, or she would cry. Whenever we were given anything from our parents or from other people, she got to choose first. Everything had to go her way, or she would tell on me. She knew very well that I would be the one who would get in trouble. She thought that the whole world revolved around her, and that everything was for her and for her only. She was very greedy, and a trouble maker. Almost eighty percent of the arguments between us were started or caused by her, but I was always the one who got punished.

After my parents left for a business trip, Agnes thought that she was the one in charge and that I had to listen to her. My mother required that we had to write to her every week, reporting to her how things were going. I had to let her read my letter before I could mail it out.

One time when our parents were away, Agnes would not finish her dinner. She asked me to finish it for her, but I did not want to. She kept asking and asking. I ignored her, but it did not work. It got uglier and uglier. She started to follow me around and would not let me do anything unless I finished the dinner for her. She tried to stop me from doing anything but what she wanted. I went to the hallway, and she followed me there. After a great deal of this, I was angry. I lost my patience and finally fought back. I slapped her and punched her. I wanted to let her know how angry I was. I fought with her because of the trouble that she made every time when our parents were out of town.

After my parents returned, they gave us two pairs of beautiful socks as a gift, one for each of us. As usual, Agnes chose first. A couple of days later, she changed her mind. She did not like hers any more and asked me to exchange.

"I do not like them, why don't you give me yours," she said to me with her socks in her hand.

"No, I like mine. Besides, you chose that yourself," I said to her.

"I changed my mind, I like yours better."

"No."

"Please."

"No."

I hid my socks. A few days later I found out that my drawers were messy. I knew that she was looking for the them.

"OK, I can not find it. Keep hiding them, and never use them. If I see that you use them, they will be mine," Agnes said with a smile on her face.

There were fewer and fewer communications between us. Sometimes we did not say a word to each other. We were no longer sisters. My parents were worried about it. They did not like to see this situation. They kept telling us that we were the only children in this family and we were sisters. If something happened to one of us, only the other one could help. I understood this, but how come my parents never examined themselves? How come they did not think that maybe they were the ones who should be blamed? They were the ones who taught Agnes this way and they never changed her behavior when she did something wrong. Agnes was spoiled. She only knew how to take and did not know how to give. She did not know how to respect others. She liked to hear good things about herself and could not stand any criticism. Unless she got everything she wanted, she would not be happy. She thought she was the best and no one else was on her mind.

Grandpa Woo. He was a certified chief engineer. He and his family had a better life than most Chinese before the Cultural Revolution.

Grandma Woo. In my memory, she was always kind and gentle to me. My grandpa and grandma Woo were my whole life. I never forget about them.

Grandma Woo was a very beautiful young lady before she married. She was the youngest daughter in her family, and was her parents' favorite daughter.

Aunt Ying and Aunt Feng were my father's sisters. They both loved me very much.

My mother's father was a lawyer and businessman. My grandmother was a house wife. As the one who held the wealth and power, my grandfather was the head of the family. His words were the final words at any time; everyone else had to obey him. In my memory, my mother's family was not so kind to me.

Chapter 8 – A Door Opens

In the spring of 1972, my mother got very excited and busy. She swapped letters with her parents, her sister, and brothers, talking about when would be a good time to go to Shanghai. I knew something big was about to happen. She told my sister and I that we had an aunt who was her oldest sister, living in the United States with her husband and two daughters. All of our relatives were planning to meet her in Shanghai when she flew in from Detroit, Michigan. My aunt Chen was coming to visit for the first time since she left China as a student.

My mother made new clothes for us, and gave us a good hair cut. We took a ship to Wuhan few days later, and met with Aunt O and two of her sons. They decided that my mother and Aunt O's older son should take the train to go to Shanghai first. Agnes and I were to continue the rest of the trip with Aunt O and her younger son by ship. On the way to go to Shanghai, my cousin was not very nice to us. As his mother, Aunt O was on her son's side. For the first time in my sister's life, she experienced what it was like to be looked down on.

In Shanghai, we had a family reunion. Everybody was there. My grandparents bought the best food, fresh vegetables, and fresh fruits. There were some strangers that sat with us when we were talking with our visitors. They were the people that the government sent to keep an eye on us, since the government wanted to know what we were talking about. Aunt Chen was so different compared to the rest of us. Her hair style was different and she dressed differently. She wore boots, a type of shoes that I had never seen before. I was so interested in everything about her.

We took Aunt Chen to walk around to parks and other places in Shanghai. One day, we went to the zoo. It was crowded and people were everywhere. It was hard for children to get close enough to watch the animals. Aunt Chen found a spot next to the fence and asked who would like to go. I raised my hand. She let me go to her and put her arms around me. Then she picked me up, put me on a high place, and took a picture of me. It was such an exciting thing that happened to me. She did not realize how much I appreciated her, and how much it meant to someone like me. Of all of the children, Aunt Chen picked me, and only me. I loved that feeling.

Aunt Chen also brought us gifts. The gifts, from the United States, were ones which none of us had ever seen before. A calculator, tissues, lip moisturizer, and a radio with two speakers were all wonders to me, but were things that Americans used everyday. After we came back home, my father took them out to show to the neighbors.

After this visit, my family started to think about immigration. But nothing happened until Mao Tsetung died in 1976, and the Cultural Revolution started to come to an end. Things started to change in 1976, and the Chinese government cracked open the door to the West which had been locked for many, many years. The Chinese people started to see the things from the West. We could listen to the Western music from the radio, watch foreign movies in the movie theatres, or watch American dance on TV. It was a huge change for the Chinese people.

A few years later, Aunt Chen came to visit for the second time. At this time, she brought her younger daughter with her, my cousin who was born in the United States. Unfortunately, my sister and I could not meet with her this time because we were still in school. They brought us many American style clothes which I liked very much. The clothes were so unusual. The colors and the designs were so different.

It was a time in China where young Chinese people started to dress themselves like an American. They would go to the barber shop to curl their hair, or dye their hair yellow. They also would wear imported jeans and sun glasses. I could feel the admiring looks from the other kids every time when I would wear those clothes. It really made me feel good. For a long time before 1976, the Chinese people were only allowed to wear black, gray, or navy. Everyone's clothes before then were so similar, and seemed just like uniforms.

Aunt Chen offered us a chance for immigration. My mother refused because she did not know what life was going to be like if we moved to the United States. Two years later, my grandparents immigrated. Aunt O, Uncle Frank and Uncle George were thinking about applying for a visa.

This time, my mother made up her mind that she was going to leave, too.

The process was long. My parents went to the police department to fill out forms. After that, we had nothing to do but to wait for a long time.

Meanwhile, I graduated from high school. I did not pass the test for entering college. But my life was getting a little better. My parents stopped spanking me. I signed up for some evening classes, and planned to take the college test again in the next year.

A year later, Uncle Frank and his family left. After that, Aunt O and her sons left. They could leave right away because they got a job in the United States. Uncle George and we were still waiting.

We finally got an answer from the police department. They asked my parents to go there for interviews. From this day on, my parents had to go to police department once every few weeks. It became my job to cook lunch. Sometimes I had to cook part of the dinner. I still did all the housework that I supposed to do.

Uncle Frank sent us many tapes with American music and we listened to them all the time. My mother invited her friends over more often since everyone enjoyed the music from the West. They talked about President Nixon, about Secretary of State Henry Kissinger, about the Republican Party and the Democratic Party, and everything that was happening in the United States. It was interesting to me. I learned something about the new country that I was going to from their conversations.

We were eventually allowed to leave the country. Now my parents had to apply and fill out the forms for the company that they worked for. It was another long process.

My grandfather sent us a letter. In the letter, he told us what we needed to prepare. He also suggested that I should get a job, not to make money, but to gain some life experiences.

My parents worked at the headquarters of their company. They helped me to get a job in one of the factories far away from home. On the other hand, they sent my sister to Shanghai to learn English with one of our cousins. Their teacher was the English tutor that my grandfather hired to teach my mother and her sisters English when they were children. This lady kept a very good relationship with my mother's family for all these years.

I finally got the freedom that I always dreamed about. The factory was located far away from home. The machines operated 24 hours a day. All of the workers were split into three groups. One group worked from 7:00am till 3:00pm, another group worked from 3:00pm till 11:00pm, and the third group worked from 11:00pm till 7:00am. Everyone took turns every two days. In order to control me, my parents required me to go home every two days.

It was the happiest time in my life. All the workers were young people about my age. I especially liked to work in the afternoon or night schedule because all the bosses were gone, and the whole department was ours. We even played hide and seek since there were many places to hide.

The bosses did not trust us. They would take turns to check on us at different times. It was no big deal. We had someone watching them, too. As soon as we found out that one of the old men was on his way, we would put out a signal, and then everyone would be on their best behavior.

I freely spent the money that I earned. I would go to a restaurant for lunch with some of the people that I worked with or bought snacks. We worked all night and would climb the mountain and have a picnic together the next morning. We were not tired at all even though we went without any sleep. I also bought some fabric and had someone make some fancy clothes for me; clothes just like every young girl on the street. Of course, those clothes and high heel shoes were only used when I lived there. I would take a shower after work, dress beautifully, and then go window shopping with my friends. We girls did it a lot. I did not need any plans, did not need any goals, other than to just walk on the street, enjoying the night view. I was no longer afraid; no longer did I have to watch my mother's face all the time and no one looked at me with scorn. I thought that I was living in heaven.

It would take me hour and half to walk to work. I could take the bus, but I chose not to. By bus, it would take almost two hours to get there, and waiting in the bus station wasted too much time. In order to get there as soon as possible so that I could play with my friends, I ran almost the whole way. Over time, I went home less and less. Then I would stay at my friend's house.

I was like a bird which was locked up too long. As soon as I was free, I never wanted to go home again. My parents were angry with my behavior, but there was nothing that they could do. They could no longer follow me to work, just like the way they used to do when I was in school. I could tell from their body language that they were angry with me every time when I visited home. They wanted to say something, but did not. It was a wonderful feeling. This wonderful time lasted for a year.

In 1984, five years after we applied for immigration, we finally got the approval from both countries. It was time to go to Beijing for visas. Uncle George's father-in-law lived in Beijing and welcomed our family to stay with them. We stopped by Shanghai to meet with my sister first, then we went to Beijing together. It was the end of December, about three weeks after my birthday. I could not go to America with my parents at this time because I was considered an adult. My parents and my sister got their visas and left. They had to find the job and prove that they made enough money to support me, and then I could get a visa and go, too.

I stayed with my mother's aunt in Shanghai for this year. She was a very nice lady. Her daughter and son-in-law were very nice to me too. They did not have any children. Every day after her daughter and son-in-law went to work, I stayed home with her. My mother signed me up for an English class in the evening and asked them to supervise me. I did not know anyone in Shanghai and could not go anywhere. During the day I studied English in my room. After dinner I went to English class. This was my everyday life. It was so boring.

I could not live in this situation too much longer and I had to find a way to do something else. I talked them into letting me do some housework such as cooking. I got a chance to go grocery shopping with my mother's aunt every morning, and Wednesday was my turn to cook anything I wanted. It was not enough for me. I was young and had a lot of energy. When I tried to do something else they would tell me to study.

"Your mother wanted you to study English. Do not waste any time."

They did not have any children, and did not know how to encourage me, or find a effective way to reach me.

I borrowed novels from uncle Zong's wife. She was a school teacher, and could get the novels from the school library. I locked myself in my room and read the novels instead of studying.

I told them that the English class started at 6:30 pm. Actually it started at 7:00. I wanted to walk to school instead of taking the bus. It was the only free time that I could walk on the street, look around, look in the store windows, or just breathe fresh air. I just wanted to relax and do something else instead of studying all the time.

Sunday was the day to visit my grandma. I left as soon as I got up and came back at 10:00 pm. I brought some small gifts for her and enjoyed her love for the day. During this year my grandma told me more things about Uncle Zong who did not treat her well. I did not like him and I did not like the way that he treated my grandma. But I could not say anything to him. In my heart I looked down upon him.

He was so handsome when he was young, got a lot of spending money from my grandpa, and dressed himself well. After my grandpa passed away, no one gave him money any more. He became a totally different person. He smoked too much and all his teeth turned yellow. He said it was his only hobby, and asked us to stop pressuring him to quit smoking. His hair was always messy. He had completely changed.

Uncle Zong and my sister were two people in my family who were spoiled. They were a negative example for me. But a negative example can be just as good as a positive example. In this case it woke me up, and helped me to see the bad results of being a spoiled child. I saw that a spoiled child was not going to have a happy life. They would get used to being the one in the center of attention, have no concerns about other people, nor would they know how to share. They became very greedy and would only take and never give. I promised myself that I would not spoil my children if I had a chance to marry someone in the future.

I learned to not be afraid to let children do something that they can handle. They can clean their rooms, set up the dinner table, take out the garbage, or learn how to earn money. Children will learn how to appreciate money if they earn their allowance, and not just have money given to them like my uncle.

In the summer, Aunt Ying invited me to stay with her family for a week. She lived in Nanging which was a beautiful city. She invited my grandma, too, but her schedule was three weeks behind mine. I really wanted to go with my grandma, but I just could not wait any longer and went by myself. A week passed by quickly and I was not ready to go back. Aunt Ying asked me to stay for another week. I struggled. I wanted to, but I was afraid that my mother's aunt would tell on me. I still decided to stay. I did not care any more. I wanted to enjoy life with the ones who loved me. Besides, it could be the last chance to do so.

My grandma showed me many of her old pictures. I asked her if I can keep some of the pictures and she agreed. I am glad that I did that. They are some of my most precious treasures today

In January, 1985, I received a letter from the American embassy. They scheduled me for an interview. I went to Beijing to meet with Uncle George's son. We were the last family members who were still in China, because we were both too old last year when our parents received their visas.

I visited Tiananmen Squire, which is the size of 60 soccer fields and is presently the heart of China. Tiananmen can be translated as the gate of heavenly peace. I also visited The Forbidden City where all the emperors had lived since the Ming Dynasty. It is rumored to have over 9,999 rooms, and is surrounded by a 10 meter high wall. All of the buildings had red walls and green roofs. I also got to see some of the treasures that used to be owned by the royal family.

I also visited the royal garden which surrounded a lake. In the middle of the lake, there was a special building, surrounded by the lake, and only accessible from a bridge. Emperor GuangXu was under house arrest by empress ChiXi in this building. Because the winter was very cold, the lake was frozen over. It was safe to walk on the surface; I walked from this building to the other side of lake, and could see the ice was dark green. But I did not get the chance to go to Great Wall because it was too cold and too windy.

Chapter 9 – A New Life in America

I flew to the United States with my cousin. It was the turning point in my life. From now on, I would live in the United States, probably for the rest of my life.

After I arrived at San Francisco International Airport, I said goodbye to my cousin. I was going to Detroit and he was going to New Orleans. I became lost in this huge airport; I was there all by myself. It was a big challenge to a girl like me. I found the English that I learned in China was no use at all. A man in uniform walked toward me and asked,

"Hi, where are you from?"

". . . . ." I stared at him.

"Where are you going?"

". . . . ."

"Do you need any help?"

". . . . . "

He walked away. A minute later, he came back with an Asian man. With this Asian man's help, I answered all the questions. On the way to go to the gate, I was surprised how kind American people were. They helped me to carry my luggage, and showed me the right way to go to the gate. On the airplane to go to Detroit, the man who sat next to me tried to talk to me, but I could not understand a word that he said.

My parents and Aunt Chen's husband picked me up from the airport. On the way home, I saw a street view which was totally different from the street view that I was familiar with. I saw McDonalds, Pizza Hut, and other little shops for the first time.

My parents and my sister lived in a small house in the middle of a huge yard, with two bedrooms, a living room and a kitchen. There were many apple trees, and a beautiful wooden shed with grape vines all around it. This was the house that Uncle and Aunt Chen had bought for the relatives who came from China. Aunt O lived in this house for a couple of years. After she was hired by a bilingual school in downtown Detroit, she moved into an apartment near the school.

The next day I went to Farmer Jack, a local grocery store, with my parents. The store was so big and clean. The fresh vegetables and the fresh fruit looked so juicy. The big and fat yellow bananas made me so hungry. I had two or three banana every day for almost half year, until I grew tired of them.

My parents drove me around town and to downtown Detroit. They showed me the apartment building that they lived in for the last year. We walked around Greektown. I was so interested by everything in the little shops. They were so colorful and beautiful. Everything was so interesting to me.

We also visited Aunt Chen and Aunt O. Uncle Frank and Uncle George moved to New Orleans a few years earlier. I met my cousins who were born in America. But we could not converse because I did not speak good English and they did not speak Chinese.

I saw so many cars on the street. Everyone drove and no one walked. I realized that driving was important in this country. My parents and my sister had received their driver's licenses already. My sister worked in a Chinese restaurant in downtown Birmingham. One day my father and I went to pick her up. My father drove me around the subdivisions. I loved those Victorian style houses. They were so much like the ones in fairy tales.

Life was very hard for a new immigrant. I did not speak good English, did not have any money, and could not drive. Also I did not have a college education, did not have a job, and did not know the culture and the lifestyle of this new country.

With Uncle Chen's help, my mother was hired by the company that Uncle Chen worked for. Her Chinese engineering certificate was not approved. She was hired because of her 30 years of engineering experience and her English language skill.

My father did not speak very good English. He was hired in a Chinese restaurant. He worked 12 hours a day for 6 days a week. In Chinese society, a white collar job is considered a high skilled job. That job can make people envious because it says that you are highly educated, and that your family can afford to send you to college. A blue collar job is considered a lowly job. As a highly educated and experienced senior engineer, it bothered my father for the rest of his life to work in a restaurant.

In America, there are many highly educated Chinese people who have immigrated here. They are engineers, doctors, or are in other high positions before they came here. They gave up everything that they had in China and immigrated in order to have a better life, freedom, and a better chance for their children which was impossible for them to have in China. Like my father, some of them speak little to no English, and their experiences in China do not count for anything here. They work in restaurants or other jobs which do not require a college degree. They have no entertainment, few friends, few relatives, and they work hard. They save all the money they can and then send their children to college for a better education. After their children graduate from college and get a dignified job, then their American dream will have come true.

I was taking English classes in Aunt Chen's school. She had to come to pick me up every morning or my father had to take me there. Someone had to take me anywhere that I needed to go, so my father started to complain.

"When are you going to learn to drive? How long do I have to be your servant?" he shouted at me when he was not in a good mood.

"Everyone in the family is doing something for you. Your sister picks you up and drops you off. Can you imagine how tired that makes her?"

They said something like this to me in order to let me know that I was nothing without them.

My sister took me to the immigration office in downtown Detroit to get a social security card. In the office, I had to fill out many forms. There were so many things that I did not know about such as zip codes, occupancy, and other things.

"What were you doing the last whole year in China? You were supposed to learn English. And is this all you learned?" she sounded like my mother and a scornful look was on her face. After she answered my question, she turned her head to look somewhere else. I pretended that I did not see this but I was sure that the person who sat next to me must have seen this very clearly.

We were the last ones to arrive in the United States. To my other relatives, we were the ones who did not know anything. Their lives were on the right track, so Aunt Chen and Aunt O were all over us. They treated us like we were stupid, but really we just were not aware of all of the American customs or the ways that Americans acted. When we visited Aunt O, she always criticized us and made us feel bad. The scornful looks made us feel that we were nothing and worthless. She was treated the same way by Aunt Chen when she arrived here fresh off the boat. Now it was her turn to treat us this way in order to make herself feel better.

Under such pressures, my mother's volcanic personality again erupted. She would yell if anything did not go her way. She would yell after we came back from visiting Aunt O. She would yell after having a bad day at work. She just took out all her frustration on her own family. One time, my father could not stand it any more and slept in the car for the night. "Get out this house and I never want to see you again," was what she yelled at me when things were not going right. I moved from room to room or I had to stand in the garage for hours to avoid her.

It was time to think about what I should do with my life. A friend of Aunt Chen's was paralyzed in an accident. They were looking for someone who could take care of him when his wife was out. Aunt Chen thought that I could handle this job. Besides, the wife was an English teacher before she was retired.

I was required to stay in their house from Monday through Friday. I lived in the basement and did not have much to do during the day. The old couple had a housekeeper who cleaned their house for them once a week. I did not need to cook either. I spent most of the time studying English in the basement. My job was to be there with the husband when the wife was at her friend's house.

My mind was still a Chinese mind; I thought of everything in a Chinese way. I did not know how to ask for payment so the old couple took advantage of me. I trusted them so much since they were Aunt Chen's friends, and took whatever they gave me. They said they would give me twenty dollars cash for spending money, and would give me more at the end of each week. Of course, they never gave me the "more" that they promised. So twenty dollars became my weekly payment.

I appreciated this opportunity. There was no way that someone like me could find a job. I did my best and never complained. I watered the garden, and cleaned the swimming pool which was very difficult. I talked to the old couple and told them about the life in China. I enjoyed the Chinese food she cooked. I also met their daughters, their sons-in-law and their grandchildren. They were very nice to me. I used the little English skills that I had to talk to their granddaughter about the TV show "All My

Children." The old couple allowed me to sit with them at the dining table if there were no visitors.

My father started to teach me to drive. He took me to an empty parking lot where I practiced in the morning. A few weeks later, he took me to a subdivision to practice. I had a directional problem which I did not know about when we were in China. I would get lost easily in the subdivisions. My father did not have this problem. Because of this, he thought everyone else did not have the problem. He was so angry every time when I turned in the wrong direction. He told me how stupid I was. We always went to the same subdivision every time and some neighbors remembered us. One day after I got lost again, my father lost patience and started yelling in the car. He told me that he was going to slap me if I turned in the wrong direction again. Soon after that we saw a police car coming toward us in our direction. The policeman was staring at us from his car. I knew one of the neighbors saw when my father yelled at me and called the police. The policeman did not stop us, but my father was scared. We went home after that.

We did not know American laws and we did not know that it was against the law to beat someone.

After I went back to the old couple's house at the beginning of the week, the life there was still boring. I did not learn any English at all. We spoke Chinese most of the time. She was not going to sit down with me and teach me English.

One day, something happened to me and I decided to quit. On one Friday afternoon, she forgot to give me the twenty dollars before I left her house. I told my mother after I got home. My mother told me that I should have asked when I was there. She told Aunt Chen about this. After a weekend of consideration, I decided to quit. The next Monday, I went to the old couple's house, and she told me that she remembered paying me and that I must have forgotten about it.

I told her that I would like to quit. It made her nervous. She tried to persuade me to stay and promised to raise my payment. She said that she would write me a check from now on, but I did not accept. A few days later she told Aunt Chen that I was trying to cheat her out of an extra twenty dollars. A few years after I quit, I heard from other people who worked for them that the couple could not keep anyone there because the wife kept the payment as low as possible.

I began to follow my sister to the restaurant where she worked. I watched her very carefully to see how to do everything. A couple of weeks later, I started to do some of the things that I could handle, such as taking away the dishes after the customers have finished with their dinner, cleaning the tables, or filling up the water for the customers. I listened very carefully to the conversation between my sister and her customers, and learned how to take food orders.

Five months after I arrived in the United States, I was on my own. I was hired at the same restaurant for which my father worked. I worked Monday evening and Tuesday evening. There were so many new things to learn. I had only heard of Coca-Cola and Pepsi when I was in China. Now I had to learn Diet Coke, Dr. Pepper, 7-Up, and others. I had to learn salt, pepper, MSG, and vegetable oil in English. I had to learn to serve properly. But I was happy. I got a job and could earn money now. Hopefully nobody would say that I was useless from now on.

The first year was very difficult and I made many mistakes. I could not understand customer's requests. Sometimes the customer did not want certain vegetables in the dish that they ordered, and wanted something else instead. It confused me. I served the wrong entree. I could not remember the name of the cocktail that the customer ordered. My boss was angry when I took the wrong order. I was yelled at a lot. Chinese bosses like to shout at their employees, in order to show how powerful they were. It happened in several restaurants that I worked for in my later life. The more I was shouted at, the more it made me nervous and the more mistakes I would make. I almost got myself fired.

Meanwhile I was taking English classes at a local school. It was free. In that school, I not only learned English and learned American songs, but I also learned other things that Americans do on a daily basis. We went to a picnic at the end of each semester, and had lunches that Americans had everyday like hot dogs, chips, pizza, and all kinds of soda. These were all new experiences for me.

After three semesters in that school, I signed up for an English class in a local community college. It cost $700 per term; each term was seven weeks. It was the class that was set up for foreign students who had a student visa. Everyone had to pass an English test before they could take any more classes at this college. I was not included because I had a green card. But I did not know this and no one in the office told me anything about it. They wanted to keep me there and have me keep paying them for school. It was very expensive for me, but my parents paid for this class. But there was no way someone like me could pass the English test after just two terms. I stopped going to the class. After I talked to a counselor, I took one math class, just to give it a try; I failed because of my English problem.

Chapter 10 – Learning About the New Country

I decided to stop taking any classes for a few years and work full time in the restaurant. I could then save up some money, and learn English by talking to the customers. There were many older returning customers who liked to stay after lunch. It was the perfect opportunity for me. Those older folks were very nice to me after I told them that I did not speak good English. They spoke slowly when they talked to me and explained to me over and over again until I completely understood. They also wrote down the word for me if I did not understand. They smiled to me, just like my grandpa and grandma. I enjoyed talking to them very much. And they tipped me very well.

One time, a customer asked for an ash tray and I did not know what an ash tray was.

"The thing that people use to carry other things is called tray," he pointed at the tray that I used to carry food.

"The tray which is for ash is called an ash tray," he put his hands underneath the cigarettes and smiled at me.

My English was getting better and better. I talked to customers about everything. I told them about my life, and asked them any questions that I had. I did not take any wrong orders and improved my service skills after working there for a while. I started to have some self confidence.

I worked over fifty hours a week. My boss let me work on the weekend which was the busiest time of the week. Only the experienced waiters were allowed to work during the weekends and I could make more money then, too. My boss had one daughter and two sons; they had immigrated to the United States about ten years before we did. He used to work for his brother-in-law for many years and then opened his own restaurant later. His son and brother-in-law also worked in the restaurant. He was an old-minded Chinese man; he always seated the customers who tipped well in his son's and brother-in-law's section. He told me that a girl did not need to make too much money. He thought all the money that I earned was going in to my savings account and that my parents covered all my living expenses.

In Chinese society, the older immigrants looked down on the new ones. After the new ones had been here a while, they would in turn look down on the people who came after them. My boss was no different. He would make fun of me because I was new, had no experience, and did not have much money. Some Chinese people like to judge others by the type of house they live in, how well they dress, and the type of cars they drive. Chinese people can be very materialistic. The daughter and her mother talked about Gucci hand bags, Rolex watches and other brands of which I had never heard. They wore 24k pure gold jewelry. I did not know any of these things. I could see the disdain in their eyes. I was not happy but I was not angry. My childhood experience taught me very well how to ignore mean things that other people did to me or said to me. This method protected me once again.

My boss's daughter was not nice to a new employee like me. So much like her father, she would criticize me:

"You always speak Chinese. When are you going to learn English?" she asked me when I spoke Chinese.

"You are Chinese. Why are you speaking English? Trying to show off?" she asked when I spoke English.

The cocktails were hard for me to remember; there were so many different kinds. Some were mixed with juice and some mixed with soda.

One night, a couple came for dinner. He ordered scotch on the rocks. I knew this one. She ordered a screwdriver.

I brought the drink for the husband. After they ordered the dinner, the wife pointed out her drink from the menu:

"Don't forget my drink, please," she reminded me.

"Oh, I am so sorry. I didn't know that a screwdriver was a drink. I thought that you are a school bus driver. It was why I did not bring your drink," I explained to her.

They both laughed so hard that they could not say a word.

"I was just hired about a year ago and I am still learning. I was wondering why you told me that you are a school bus driver."

They laughed some more.

They tipped me very well after dinner. That night I learned a new cocktail and never forget about a screwdriver again.

As time passed by, my English got better. My service skills were getting much better, too. I remembered all the vegetables in each entree, so I could answer any questions the customers may have. Sometimes I even helped the customers order their dinner depending on their personal health or their personal tastes.

Before computers were widely used in the restaurants, the only tool that we had to use was the calculator. I forced myself to add the final total price together in my mind and then used the calculator to double check it. It sharpened my mind especially when six or eight people came in for dinner as a group.

I enjoyed doing this job. It gave me the chance to talk to people. I also learned a lot of people skills that have helped me in my later life. I learned how to solve problems without asking my boss each time, especially when it was the busiest time of the day. I learned how to handle difficult customers who were very picky. I learned how to keep my customers happy which would enable them to tip me, and keep my boss happy. It freed me.

I worked behind the bar in another Chinese restaurant a few years later. I learned how to make cocktails, and learned how to handle the attacks from some of the unfriendly customers. All of this was very valuable experience for me.

I have heard people complain about how hard it is to work in a restaurant. It was very true. It also depends on how one looks at it. If anyone has a positive attitude, this job can turn into a very rewarding experience. From this job, I learned so much about people skills, and other things that I could not learn from classes in school.

I had some customers who requested me to be their waitress only whenever they came in for dinner.

There was one family who came in for lunch every Saturday. The father and mother had two daughters, Theresa and Linda, who were about my age. We got to know each other very well over time, and one day the two girls asked if I could go out with them. Of course, I loved to. They were members of a local singles club. I started to go to the dances at the club with them, to go camping with them, and do other things that I had never done before. It gave me a chance to get to know American people and their life on a daily basis. I kept a good friendship with them for many years.

Even today, I am surprised that I was not afraid to try things that to me were completely unknown. I know there are many Chinese who are not comfortable entering American society even after they have lived here for a long time. I think it is about my outlook on life, and that I was able to be open, positive, and happy, even with all my bad experiences as a child. Thinking about the things that I like to do, such as ballet, or looking at the blue sky filled with white clouds, would make me happy. It is a gift from God and has helped me and supported me in my life in many ways.

I thought that my English was good enough to take another class. I signed up for one math class at a local community college, just gave it a try, and ended up getting a B+. It was such a happy time in my life. It meant that I was ready for a college education in English.

I talked to my father about supporting myself and giving them some money each month. After a discussion, we agreed that I would give my parents $550 every month. It was half of my father's mortgage payment. In those days a very nice apartment would rent monthly for $400. The reason I wanted to do so was because I wanted to tell my parents that I could support myself, and I was not as useless as they thought I was. But my parents did not treat me any better. They took the money, and still treated me as bad as before. They thought that since they raised me, that now it was my turn to return everything. Some Chinese parents did this to their children; it was called in Chinese "returning the raise." I did not mind to pay them back; I would be free after I paid them off, and they would no longer own me.

The car was acting up, especially during the winter. The next year, the engine died many times, and I had to restart it over and over before it would go again. I told my father that I would like to buy a new car. My father thought about it and suggested that he and I buy one together. I did not agree.

"No," I said to him.

"A new car is expensive, depending on the type of car that you want to buy."

"I know. But still, either I pay the whole thing or I pay nothing."

My father agreed.

I had a reason for doing it. My sister was very greedy. If we bought a new car, she would be the one who would drive it all the time. If my father and I bought the car together, she still could find any excuse to drive it. In order to stop that, I wanted to make sure that the car would be mine, and mine only. I wanted to be sure that only my name was on the title. What happened later was exactly what I thought would happen.

After I bought a new 1988 Grand Am, my father said to me, "I will pay for the gas, and cover the insurance. But from now on, everyone in this family has the right to drive it."

I agreed and gave a car key to each of them.

Just like I thought, my sister drove my car all the time without asking for permission. I did not say anything at the beginning because I was waiting for the right moment to do so.

A few days later my sister took my car out in the afternoon. I had an evening class that day and I needed the car. I decided to say something this time. She came back and a few minutes later, she was ready to go out again.

"You are not going to take my car any more. You have to ask for my permission if you need it from now on." I said to her.

"But I need it right now," she looked at me.

"No, you do not, since you did not ask for my permission. You figure a way to go to the place that you need to go. It is not my business."

"You are mean. You are my sister. Why can't you let me use when I need it?" she started to get angry.

"Really? Am I your sister? How come you never treated me like a sister before? Think about it yourself. You didn't treat me good since we were young. Now I am your sister because you need my car."

She never took my car after that, but from then on, our arguments got louder and louder.

I paid off the car in two years.

My mother was still on my sister's side, did her favors, and gave her many things. Their behavior never changed.

My mother gave us gold chains one day, one for each of us. It was the first piece of real gold jewelry that I ever had. I did not want to wear it to work, so I put it safely away. Two days later, my mother said to me, "Why don't you give it back to me if you aren't going to wear it? That way I could wear and enjoy it."

I trusted her and give it back to her.

The next day, I saw the chain on my sister's neck. I was so angry because of the way I was cheated. I gave it back to my mother because she told me that she was going to wear it. I would never have done it if I knew that she was going to give it to my sister. There was no point in saying anything to them. I bought another one for myself. I felt better wearing my own one anyway.

I was thinking about moving out. I did not know when would be the right time, or how to do it. It was a big challenge for someone like me. All the things that I did for my family, helping my parents to pay the mortgage payment, buying my own car, paying my own college tuition, were just not good enough. I never remembered having heard any positive things from them. They never said thanks to me. I did not buy much for myself, but instead saved up money in my father's saving's account, so he could use it when he needed. He agreed that he would return it to me if I needed it in the future. My parents updated their cars, bought new furniture from the House of Denmark, an expensive local furniture store. They had a twelve year mortgage and paid it off in six years with my help. But my parents never changed their attitude toward me. They were too proud to change, for it would make them lose face.

When my uncle Frank and Uncle George came to visit, they just could not believe their eyes. Every time when they came, they saw something new that my parents had bought. They did not know how my parents could afford to buy all these new things. Uncle Frank bought a house before us that was around the same price. Twelve years later, he was still paying on the mortgage. They drove secondhand cars and they did not have any expensive furniture. I heard them ask my parents where they got the money from. Finally my parents told them that I paid them $550 each month, along with making my own car payment, and also my own college tuition. I could see by the surprised looks on everyone's faces that this was not what they expected. A girl who was the stupid one in everyone's mind did all this by herself? At this moment, I felt that I was going to cry, but I did not.

I believed in myself even more, and had a lot more confidence. I knew that my relatives looked down on my father and I, because we worked in a Chinese restaurant. To them, it was a cheap job, and only lowly people worked such jobs. Their minds were still Chinese minds, even though they had been in the United States for many years. My mother felt shame in front of her parents, brothers, and sisters because her husband and her daughter worked in a restaurant.

One summer, my grandmother came back from visiting China. She bought gifts for all her grandchildren. The gifts for Aunt Chen's children were the most expensive ones. Then, lesser expensive gifts were given to Uncle Frank's sons and Uncle George' sons. After that, even less expensive gifts for Aunt O's sons, with the ones for my sister and me the cheapest. Grandma actually told us all the prices for the gifts. It was the way that my grandmother treated her children and grandchildren. Everything that happened in my family made sense to me now. It made sense to me why my mother was not happy about her position in her family. It made sense to me why my mother treated my sister and me so differently. It was her way of revolting against her parents that she would favor the youngest one since her parents favored the oldest one.

I still had a difficult time in college. I chose Accounting to be my major. It was not because I wanted to. It was actually my mother's idea. I was not really interested in anything, so my mother suggested that an accounting major might not be a bad idea. So I did it.

Accounting required a lot of reading. Besides all the accounting classes, there were the other business classes, too. It was very difficult for me. There were strange, new words all over every page of the books. I brought a dictionary with me all the time, even during exams. In order to graduate as early as possible, I started taking two classes each semester while still working full time. I dropped the classes many times, because I could not get good enough grades. I did not want to get "C's" and "D's" all the time, so I retook the classes over and over again, until I could get an "A", or a "B." I still remember that one of my Accounting professors was surprised to see me taking his class again and again. He probably did not see such students too often. Maybe I should have explained to him that it was my problem, not his.

Meanwhile I was still working in the restaurant. For seven years straight I studied and worked. No weekends, no holidays, no vacations.

I attended a local Chinese Bible church, not to worship the Lord, but to meet some new people. I did not know anything about Jesus, or the Bible, or religion. I could not understand the preaching of the pastor, who used English and Cantonese when he was speaking. Cantonese was a Chinese dialect that I did not understand. My English was good enough for daily conversation, but was not good enough for reading the Bible.

I always felt sleepy when the pastor was preaching, but at church I got a chance to meet and know other people. At this time, I had so many questions about God and the Bible. I did not understand why God let terrible things happen to us if he is so powerful and knows everything like the way that the Bible told us. I did not feel that I was protected. Instead I felt that I was suffering; I thought that God let suffering happen and did nothing about it. I did not understand why God did not punish the people who did bad things. It did not look like God existed at all.

The people in the church told me it would take me some time to understand the Bible. They gave me a Chinese language Bible, and prayed with me. They told me that everything that God said to us, and everything that God had promised us was in this book. I read it a little, and then put it away. It was too hard for me.

I was baptized with some other people that I got along with. I did not fully understand what it meant until many years later.

Aunt O and my mother started to worry about marriage for me. I was still single, and did not know where or how to look for a boyfriend. Aunt O introduced a couple of boys who were her friends' sons. But they were from out of state, and we did not have a chance to get to know each other.

There was a Chinese man that we knew from a long time ago, who helped us when we just immigrated to this country. He and his wife came to visit several times. We lost contact for many years after that. I almost forgot about him, until I became friends with a Chinese girl I met in college. One day, she mentioned that she would like to introduce a Chinese man to me. Soon this man and I started dating. When I took him home to introduce him to my family, my mother pulled me aside and told me that she recognized him as the one that we met from a long time ago. She said that she did not feel right about this, and asked me to stop contacting him because she remembered this man was married.

I did. A few days later, my friend asked me what was happening, so I explained to her. She told me it was a misunderstanding. This young man was the nephew of that man that we met from long time ago, and they looked like each other. I explained it to my mother after I got home. All of the sudden, my mother was very interested in this young man.

"Call him, invite him for dinner. I would like to talk to him, and get to know him." She said to me.

"But I stopped talking to him, and stopped answering his phone calls just the way that you told me to," I answered.

"No big deal, just call him."

"No, I am not going to," I refused again, and this whole thing was over.

My sister invited a Chinese couple home one day, and we all got long very well. They came and visited a few times after that. They looked like a loving couple to us until one day the husband came alone. He told us that he was divorced. It was a big surprise to all of us.

Every time when this man came to visit, my mother and sister always had some excuses to leave the room, and leave us alone. I knew that she wanted me to date this man.

He worked for the Ford Motor Company, and had a PhD degree. He was exactly the type of man that my mother liked: highly educated, good job, worked for a large company. If one day in the future, her daughter married this man, it would make her look good in front of the entire family. She could proudly tell everyone, "See, my son-in-law has a PhD degree, and he works for Ford."

In Chinese society, the parents would be so proud of their children if they could be in a high position in society, or marry someone who is in a high position. It would make the parents look good in other people's eyes, and they could enjoy the envious looks from others, especially my mother who wanted to prove something to her parents, sisters, and brothers who always looking down on her. She wanted to prove that she could do good things just like anyone else in this family. If she could raise her daughters properly, then she could be in the same position as anyone else in this family. But she swallowed too much bitterness over the years, and had waited too long to hear praise from her parents. She did not know how to stand up for herself or fight for herself and her own family. She completely let everyone else in her family control her life.

To my mother, this was the chance to change everything. She pushed me hard to go out with this man, and she invited him over for dinner.

But I did not enjoy going out with this man at all. First, Chinese men are not as romantic as American men. Second, this man was just divorced and was still in a bad mood about it. To a man like him, divorcing made him loose face. He may have been successful in his career, but the divorce told other Chinese that his personal live was not good at all. He was not in the mood to date.

"Hi, I will take you out tonight; I will meet you at your house in a few minutes."

"OK, I'll see you later."

This was the phone conversation; it was always so short, without feeling, and not like the phone conversations between a loving couple.

He lived in West Bloomfield which was a well-to-do suburb of Detroit. He took me to his house where my mother told me not to go. He always picked me up with a different company car each time we went out. It was his way to show off to me. However, he did not know anything about me at all, and I was not the type of person who is attracted by position or wealth. He was not an attractive man to me at all, and I could not stand him any longer.

One afternoon, I told him that I would like to stop this relationship. I planned to look for a man who would respect me and love me from his heart. I did not want someone who would judge me by the type of job that I had, check my income, or check on my family background like most of the Chinese people did.

My parents told me not to go out with any American man, because they were different from us and were from a different culture. They also told me that if I got into a American man's car, I would not know where this man was going to take me. But from my experience, I did not think that American men were that bad. At least, not everyone was like that. I asked myself that if I met the right American man in the future, would I have the courage to go out with him. I did not know.

I told my parents that I was ready to move out and that I would like to look for an apartment; I was ready to have my own life. It was a bombshell. My father and mother were both angry, and argued with me, trying to change my mind. I knew it was about losing face with other relatives and friends. In Chinese society, a young girl is supposed to stay home with her parents until she marries. If I moved out before I married, it would tell others that there were some problems in the family.

But my parents should have thought about it long ago. They knew that I was different from others, and they could have treated me better when I was younger. I was ready to get out this house now; nothing could change my mind. Anyway, they were the ones who, whenever they were not happy with me, had told me many times in the past to get out the house and that they never wanted to see me again.

My father said to me that if I decided to move out, he would stop supporting me in any way. I would be completely on my own after that point in time. He also made it clear that I should not expect to move back if I was ever in any trouble.

Chapter 11 – The Start of Independence

My friend Theresa, one of the two girls from the family who came for lunch every Saturday, offered me the opportunity to live in one of the rooms in her house. Theresa and Linda were good students in college, and had graduated from a local engineering school. Theresa worked for GM and Linda worked for Ford. Theresa had bought their parents' house after her father had moved to Traverse City upon retirement from Ford.

When I moved into Theresa's house, I was finally free. It was such a huge step in my life; I was on my own. I was holding my future in my hands, and it would all depend on what I was going to do from now on.

Since I moved into Theresa's house, it gave me a chance to know Theresa better. I had not yet learned everything about American ways. A lot of time, I still thought of things in a Chinese manner, and it caused some misunderstanding between Theresa and me. I noticed that Theresa never asked me about myself, or my family, or the reason why I immigrated to the United States. She also never told me anything about herself, or her family, or her life. If I did something that did not make any sense to her, I would get strange looks from her. She never asked me why I did it the way that I did, or explained to me the American way of doing things. Sometimes, I wished that she would explain it to me. It would help me a lot, and we could avoid some of the misunderstanding. I felt that Theresa built an invisible wall between her and me. In order to avoid some of the unnecessary problems, I controlled myself and chose not to ask too many questions. I felt that in her mind she was the landlord, and I was the tenant. I realized because of this that there was not really a deep friendship between us even though I tried to be her friend. But Theresa's parents were very friendly. They talked to me a lot more then their daughter did.

At the restaurant where I worked, Christmas was the busiest time of the year and my boss would expand the working hours for these two days. One Christmas Eve after I came back from work, her mother invited me to sit with them, and handed me a gift that she bought for me. It was so nice of her.

Linda's wedding was the first American wedding that I had attended. I got to see their ceremony in the church, and the celebration after that. It was wonderful and opened my eyes. The Chinese weddings I had been to, had been during Communist times and did not involve religion.

I had a hard time understanding conversation when Theresa and Linda invited their friends over. I could answer the questions that I was asked, but could not talk about topics like sports, politics, or the news that was on TV or from a newspaper. I could not play some of the games that they played. I was either working or studying, and did not have much time to watch TV or read the newspaper. Even if I did, I did not understand it completely.

My American friends did not realize what life was like when someone comes from a different country. Moving to another country was like being born again. It would take a long time to learn a completely different culture. I was not an American born Chinese; I was raised in Chinese culture and would have to learn everything from the very beginning. The difficulties I had in talking to my American friends were not because I did not want to talk to them, it was because I did not understand them, nor did they understand me. They were friendly to me, but deep down, I could feel that I was the outsider. I knew that I still had a long way ahead of me and a lot to learn if I wanted to successfully enter American society.

Since my family immigrated to the United States, Aunt Ying and Uncle Zong were hoping that my father could help their daughters to go to the United States for their college education, and my father thought about it for many years. After my sister married, and I moved out the house, he thought it was time to help his nieces. He talked to my mother about it, and my mother did not agree for two reasons. The first was that my father's family did not treat my mother nice when we were in China. The second reason was that my father and my mother were still working, and Aunt Ying and Uncle Zong were retired. My mother thought it was not fair to her. Besides, my father was thinking to cover all the expenses for my two cousins, which would include all the college tuition, and all of the living expenses.

My father did not involve himself in any activities besides working, and he did not read American newspapers or watch the news on TV. He had no idea what American society was all about, other than what he saw working in the Chinese restaurant. He did not know how expensive college tuition would be, especially for foreign students.

I was my father's daughter, but I had to pay my own tuition and I paid my parents $550 each month when I lived with them. My father planned to let my cousins live in his house for free, but did not have plans for getting them to school. Whether he would drive them to school or they would take driving lessons and get a car were questions that were not answered. My father planned to extend his retirement out and work for another year. He thought that the money he earned should be able to cover all the tuition, but he had not investigated the costs for two foreign students per year. His thought was that if he worked in the restaurant for one more year, that that money should cover the tuition of two foreign students for their four years of college.

My mother was very angry. From their arguments, I heard a lot of things that happened in my family that I had never heard before. I had always gotten little bits of stories from each of my relatives over the years, and now I started to put them together to get the big picture. I started to understand my parents' background and the reasons why they treated me so bad. People tell the truth when they are angry.

Three years after I moved out my parents' house, I graduated from Oakland Community College with my Associates Degree in Accounting. From the day I took my first math class until the day I graduated took almost ten years; it was such a difficult ten years for me. I was so excited because I did it all by myself, without any help. I did not owe any money at the time I graduated; I had paid off everything, and I was so proud. It meant so much to me and proved that I could be a success. I was not as stupid as my family thought; I was intelligent and just needed a chance.

I also learned an important lesson, which was to be independent. Someone who has gone through many difficult situations can understand how important it is to be independent of other's opinions. One should not listen to other's statements about what kind of person one is, since others do not know one's self. Individuals can be much stronger than they are often given credit for, and by studying and working hard, can achieve success.

Remember the story "The Ugly Duckling?" I was that ugly duckling. I was not cute or smart, but was different from the others, and nobody cared about me. But now I felt like a swan that could fly freely in the sky.

I had a million reasons to love this great country, the United States of America. Only this country viewed everyone equally. Only in this country does everyone have a chance to be a success. I am so proud to be an American.

I did not invite my family to attend the graduation ceremony. I did not feel comfortable to do it. The diploma was mailed to me without any celebration. Nobody said anything positive to me, it was just like nothing happened. My father said to me that he wished I could go to a university until I completed the other two years of education.

I decided to move out of Theresa's house, and to look for a small apartment. I met another American girl, Joanie, who spoke excellent Chinese. She came for dinner with her boyfriend one night, and during a conversation with the restaurant owner, she told him that she had bought a house and was looking for roommates. The owner mentioned that I was looking for an apartment. So this is how we met. I moved into Joanie's house and lived with two of Joanie's cats, Mink and Sapphire. The cats and I became best friends.

In 1994, nine years after I immigrated to United States, I flew back to China by myself to visit some of my relatives. From calling the Chinese embassy in Chicago, applying for a visa, and ordering the airplane ticket; I did it all by myself. Before the departure day, I drove to the airport to get familiar with parking, the shuttle bus, and the international terminal.

I flew to Chicago first. The Chicago airport was huge. I followed directions to the people mover to the other side of the airport, and arrived at the gate without getting lost. It was a big success for someone like me who had a terrible directional problem; I had never traveled such a huge distance by myself before.

I got on an airplane from the Chinese East Airline Company. I liked the environment that I was in. Nine years after I had immigrated to the United States, I was among Chinese again. I had a good feeling about this. Everyone around me spoke Chinese; I liked that. I got a cold the day before I left so I took cold medicine that morning before leaving. It made me so sleepy for the most of the trip. I woke up a few hours before landing. It worked out perfectly for me since the eighteen hour trip was boring.

The Chinese nation's attitude about service had not changed much since I left China. Over one hour after getting off the plane, my luggage was nowhere to be found. There was no explanation as to where it was, and no offer of any help. Finally, someone told me that it was still in Chicago, and that I could retrieve it in three days. I met Uncle Zong who had come to pick me up. It took us one hour to get home; the street was crowded, and I saw a lot more cars then before. My grandma Woo had passed away four years ago. The board between the living room which separated my grandma and Uncle Zong was gone. The whole living room looked so much bigger and brighter. This room and all the old furniture that my grandparents had left brought back to me so many of my childhood memories.

As soon as I got to Uncle Zong's apartment, I cleaned up and then went to the supermarket with him. I loved the smell in the supermarket; I used to smell it every day when I was young. Uncle Zong let me chose the vegetables that I liked for dinner. After grocery shopping, we stopped at a small restaurant for breakfast. I ordered the food that I liked when I was a child.

Every morning after Uncle Zong and his wife left for work, I went out by myself with a back pack on my back. I stood on the side of the river next to the apartment for a long time, smelled the familiar smells from this river, and watched the boats pass by. Everything was the same as before. My grandpa and grandma used to take me here many times when I lived with them. I went to HuangPu park which was my favorite one and was most beautiful area in Shanghai. This is where the HuangPu river empties into the ocean. Many buildings in this area were built by Western businessmen over one hundred years ago. The buildings are English style, Russian style, and Gothic style, and house banks, restaurants, clubs, and hotels. The HuangPu Avenue was beautifully decorated with trees and flowers. I saw American cars all over the street. But I also noticed that the air was terribly polluted. Just like Fifth Avenue in New York, Ninging Road is the biggest shopping street in Shanghai. I bought many things, but mainly clothing. I bought a lot of snacks. I bought the kind of ice cream that I loved when I was a child. I only bought the things or ate the food that I was familiar with, and ignored the new things. I had lunch in a local restaurant. I could not find the traditional foods any more. Instead there was a lot of fast food. Uncle Zong told me that I had to go to certain restaurants to find the traditional foods that I remembered. I took a lot of pictures. Shanghai had changed a lot since I left. The tall buildings were everywhere, and everywhere there was construction. But I still could figure out the way back, or I could take a cab home which I could not do when I lived here nine years ago because they were not available.

I took a five day trip to Yellow Mountain National Park with Uncle Zong's daughter. I chose to join a tour with the local people instead of a tour with foreign tourists where I could get much better service and stay in a better hotel. I just wanted to re-experience the life that I had before. People on the bus spoke Chinese, and they talked about their families. It made me feel so comfortable.

Yellow Mountain National Park is one of the most beautiful national parks in China. Several ancient famous Chinese poets wrote poems to describe the beautiful views about Yellow Mountain. My cousin and I decided to climb all the way to the top instead of taking the cable car. The line for the cable car was long and we would miss a lot of views if we took it.

We arrived and stayed in a hotel the night before we started to climb. We heard all kinds of noise from the street after dark. It was the local people doing their night activities. My cousin and I went out to the crowded street. People were selling handcrafts that they had made. They were also selling homemade goods and homemade food that they had cooked. The smell was so good. I controlled myself not to eat any of this food, because I was afraid of getting sick, even though I wanted to try some of it so badly. My cousin and I could not sleep well that night, so we sat on the bed and talked all night long.

Before we started the climb, we hired one of the local people to carry our baggage for us. The local people did this for a living. They would gather several tourists' baggage together, and climb in front of us. Then they stopped at a specific place, and waited for us. I could not believe how strong these local people were. By the time we got there, they had already waited for us for thirty minutes. We made the right decision to hire this local man; he told us that there was no way we could climb all the way up without his help. He was absolutely right.

We were there for three days. The last day, we climbed up to the top of one of the highest mountains. When we looked around, the clouds were under our feet and all of the mountains around us were in the clouds. I could see so far. I stood there, thinking only God could make all this. When someone stood here and looked around, how in the world that they could believe all of this was from nothing? How could someone not believe God was the one in charge and made all of this for us?

The hard part was coming down from the top of the mountain. The stairs were so narrow that only one person at a time could go through. It was a forty-five degree slope down.

When we arrived at a rest area, I saw the local people were selling handcrafts. I wanted to buy something, but thought about the long way down that we still had to face. I was so tired and my legs were so sore. I had to carry all the things I bought with me, if I bought them right now. So I decided to wait for the next opportunity after I got down to the bus station. What an opportunity that I missed. I never found these handcrafts again.

With my two favorite aunts, I traveled to several historical cities that I always wanted to visit but never get the chance to go to when I was a child. We took a train with air conditioning. On this train, no one was allowed to smoke, which I loved very much. We talked and enjoyed the view outside the window. I volunteered to pay for all the expenses. I wanted my aunts to enjoy a vacation for once in their lives. It was my way to thank them for all their love. They took me shopping, and helped me to bargain prices down with the local merchants. They took me to parks; we enjoyed dinners in the restaurants. I stayed in Aunt Ying's house when I was visiting Ninging. I enjoyed every minute when I was there. She bought me all kinds of food that I loved for lunch and dinner.

I was not an experienced traveler. I did not call the airport to confirm the schedule and the airplane that I was going to take on the way back. Everything was OK until I arrived in Chicago. I was supposed to go to on to Detroit, but instead the airplane took me to New York. I found out when I asked the flight attendant why the plane had not landed on time, but it was too late. Three people had checked my ticket, and no one had found the problem. I waited in the airport by myself until someone took me into a hotel. The next day, I finally was on the way home.

I was afraid to lose my passport during this trip, so I asked Uncle Zong to lock it in a drawer along with my cash. Each day I only took a little money with me when I went out. I had recorded how much I took out each time and how much I had spent every day. The day before I left China, Uncle Zong gave me back the passport and the remaining money and I found out a hundred dollar bill was missing.

Several months after I returned to the United States, I received a letter from Uncle Zong. In his letter, he told me that he had lost a lot of money gambling. He said that the gangsters would go after him if he did not return the money in a certain time. He begged me to help him out, and asked me not to tell anyone in the family. I was asked to send the money to a specified mailing address which was different from his normal mailing address as soon as possible.

I knew him well enough that I could tell he lied to me. He needed money, but did not have the nerve to ask from anyone else in the family, so I was targeted. First, I was just a simple, silly kid. Second, I lived so far away from him. Third, he asked for cash, so he could deny it if someone found out later. I sent a letter to him.

> Dear Uncle Zong—
> I was so surprised after I read your letter. You are asking for about two thousand dollars. It is a huge amount of money to me. I have to tell you the situation that I am in right now. Since I came to the United States, nobody ever helped me like this. I was on my own completely. I had to pay my college tuition, car payments, and many other living expenses. I work very hard for my own living. I could consider loaning you some money for business purposes. But I have a hard time to give you the money that I earned to help you paying off the debt that you owe in gambling. If you are really an independent man, never ask for help like the way you said in your letter and figure out a way to pay it off yourself.

I never sent the money to him.

After I came back from China, I started taking classes at Wayne State University. I did not promise myself anything, but just wanted to give it a try. The classes were much more difficult for me, and the tuition was much more expensive. I had a lot of pressure during that time.

I met an German-American man, Curt, who later became my husband. He was a friend of Joanie's boyfriend. At the beginning, I refused to go out with him when Joanie introduced him to me, because I was a little nervous. I had gone out with a couple of American men before him. They just wanted to have fun and were not serious about dating. They told me that they were not going to consider marriage until they were forty so I left them.

When Curt came into my life, I was wondering if he might be the same type as the other two that I had gone out with. But I still decided to give him a chance. I was all ready to leave him as soon as I found out that he was like one of those other men.

This time I was wrong. The more I spent time with him, the more I felt that he was a gentleman. He made me feel comfortable and relaxed, and he respected me. Just three months after I met him, from my feelings I knew that he would be the last one that I was going to date. I was tired of being single. I was tired of going out with men for whom I had no feelings. I hoped to find a man that I could depend on for the rest of my life. Life was tough for a young lady who came from a different country, only spoke some English, and had to handle everything for herself.

Joanie found a new roommate, Karen, another engineer, who worked for EDS. What was going on? Everyone in my life was engineers. Joanie was an engineer too. I was like a magnet attracting iron. I did not go to them, but they came to me. Karen had graduated from GMI Engineering & Management Institute which was one of the best engineering schools in Michigan. It was also the school from which my husband graduated.

Karen and I became friends. We both were dating, so we had a lot to talk about. We both moved into a rented house after the lease with Joanie expired.

One semester, when I was taking three classes, I reduced some of my working hours. It meant I lost part of my income. I talked to my parents and asked if I could move back for a short time.

"No," my mother said to me on the phone. "You can not afford it because you did not do your best. Everything is possible if you do your best. Besides, you left this home too long, and I do not feel comfortable to let you move back. We had too many difference in life."

I talked to Karen to see if I could pay a little less rent, and let her cover the utility cost for three months. I would be responsible for all the cleaning for this house. I would mow the law in the summer, clean the driveway in the fall, and shovel the snow during the winter. Karen agreed. Actually, she covered the utility cost for me until we both moved out of this house. I loved this way. We lived peacefully together and helped each other. Karen and I became long term friends.

Meanwhile, I was saving dimes and quarters to buy ballet tapes. I had "Swan Lake," "The Nutcracker," and "Sleeping Beauty." I watched them over and over again when I had any free time, and never grew tired of them.

Sometimes, Curt had to make presentations at Cobo Hall in downtown Detroit. Several times he met me in the cafeteria of Wayne State University and we had lunch together. One time, he even walked me to my classroom, and sat down with me for a few minutes. It always made me happy.

After a few semesters, I decided to stop taking classes. I worked too hard, and never get the chance to enjoy the life that I wanted. I did not want to spend all the money that I earned on college tuition any more. I wanted to go out and enjoy life with Curt and friends like Karen. I did not care what my parents thought of me any more. I did not care how much my parents were disappointed with me. I did not want to live my life for those people who did not help me when I needed it. I wanted to live for myself and the people who cared about me. So my college life came to an end.

Life was so much easier after I stopped going to school and paying tuition. It was a huge relief. I could work more and save all the money I earned. Curt and I went out for dinner, watched movies, and sometimes went to the mall.

Curt took me to visit his parents for two weeks during one Christmas break. They lived in Omaha, Nebraska. We drove there, over seven hundred miles from Michigan. In Omaha, he showed me the middle school that he attended when he had lived there a long time ago and showed me around the Omaha area. There were many corn fields out away from the city. It was different from Detroit.

I had American meals for two weeks straight. I missed Chinese food so much during this two week period.

In 1996, I said yes when Curt asked me to marry him. We were now engaged. The reason I said "yes" to him was because he never judged me like any of my family members. He knew that I was a waitress when he met me. He never asked how much money that I made. He never checked my family background like the way that Chinese people usually do. I think this is one of the reasons why many Chinese young ladies like to date American men.

We were looking for a church for our wedding ceremony and also to attend. We made a list of several churches from the yellow pages. Berean Bible Church was the first one on our list. We went there one Sunday morning, and have attended there ever since.

My English was much better now. I could understand the pastor's preaching. Everything from the Bible started to make sense to me. Curt was born in a Christian family. He could answer many of the questions that I had. Slowly, I started to understand the Bible and all of the things that Jesus had done for us.

Today, I finally realize the Lord was with me the whole time, had never forgotten me, and had never left me behind. Looking back, the Lord let me stay in China safely for the first year that my parents and my sister were in the United States. They lived in an apartment in downtown Detroit, and told me they were scared to live there. The people who lived next door played loud music. The rooms were dirty. My sister had to walk to school, which was not in a safe area. They could hear people shouting in the apartment. By the time I arrived, my parents had already moved into the house that Aunt Chen bought for us in Southfield, across the street from the company that my mother worked for. It was a much safer place than downtown Detroit. The Lord gave me the strength that I needed to handle everything. He was the one that protected me from other people's attacks. I thought that He did not do anything for me in the early years, but He did and I just did not see it. Later I saw that He wanted to train me to be a stronger person; difficult situations make people strong. He had certain expectations of me and trained me for this. He was the one that sent the right person to me and helped me every time when I moved. He was the one who sent my husband into my life. There is no such thing called "luck." Everything is in God's hands; He is the one in charge, not my parents, nor anyone else.

Chapter 12 – Agree or Disagree

After Curt and I were married, I moved into his one room apartment. I worked for an American restaurant named "Mountain Jack's Steak House." I liked to work there and felt comfortable. My personality fit in so well and I could joke with people in any way that I wanted. Nobody felt uncomfortable, and nobody said that I was weird. Everybody loved to joke with me, too. I loved the team that I was in; we helped each other, got along very well, and were always happy. Our general manager raised our pay because she did not want to lose us.

I had to work during the weekends and the holidays. Curt understood this, and he never complained about it. And I was getting used to working at any time, and never even thought it could cause problems.

We took some time off, traveled to Washington D.C., Toronto, and some other places. We went to the ice cream shop cross the street from our apartment one winter night. My husband took me to some of the car shows that he liked attend. He also took me to his friends' parties. I still miss this short but sweet time today.

The next year, we bought a house and my life finally started to settle down. I could call it my home and I felt safe there. After I became pregnant, I quit my job. I wanted to be a stay-at-home mom and raise my children by myself. I did not want to repeat my parents' mistakes. I wanted to watch my children grow up; their success will be my success.

My parents were disappointed about my decision. In my family, everyone had a career except me. They were disappointed because I did not go the way that they had arranged for me. They felt that they were losing control of me.

After we bought our house, my parents asked me many questions that I did not feel comfortable to answer, such as how much our house cost, how much our TV cost, or how much our cars cost. They also wanted to know Curt's salary. My parents wanted to know, and my husband asked me not to tell. It was not fun to be the one in the middle. I knew that as soon as I told my parents, then the word would spread all over the entire family.

"Is this some kind of secret? You can tell us, can't you? We are family," my mother asked on the phone.

"You want to know, and my husband asked me not to tell. It is hard for me. In this country, people do not talk about these things, and only tell their spouses. Even my in-laws do not know anything about his salary," I told her.

"I do not understand what the big deal is about telling your own parents."

"Please do not ask again. I will not tell you." I told her for the last time.

After that, my parents separated themselves from me even more. They would not tell me anything that happened in their house any more.

Since I moved out of their house, I visited my parents once every week, and called them once a week. They complained that I did not visit enough. This situation still went on after I married.

The visits with them were not happy times for my husband and me. My parents would criticize me, and argued with me most of the time when we visited them. They would not argue with me in English, and they would not argue with me when Curt was there. They did not want my husband to know that they were disagreeing with me, or that they were not happy with us. They always put a mask on when he was there.

Many times Curt did not know until we were on the way home. I was very upset in the car, and explained to him what it was all about. For the rest of the night, no one was happy. It happened too many times. We both did not like to visit them any more. It gave us a lot of pressure when the time came to go visit. We did not know what the visit would turn out to be. We mentally prepared for all the possible problems that might happen before we left our home. Sometimes, I gave them the excuse that Curt was busy and we did not go. They complained that I could go with my daughters without him if he was busy. They were dreaming; Curt would not let me visit them alone. If the visit turned into a disaster, I would still have to drive home by myself with my children. Curt would not want me to make the long drive home after a potentially bad visit. He would not want anything to happen to his family because of my parents. During these times, my parents never thought about why we did not like to visit them, and why our visits grew further and further apart.

After my mother retired, my parents bought a house in a town far away from me and my family. Agnes bought a house near them. Since I was young, they were always in one group, and I was always separate from them. After my sister was married, and I was later married, things were still going that way. My brother in-law, Charles, used to work in the same company that my mother worked. Now they lived so close to each other. It was the way that my parents liked.

By talking to my parents' realtor, Charles and Agnes found his childhood dream, which was a thirteen acre wooded lot. He wanted to buy it and build a house on this land, but they could not afford it. After his parents refused to help, they asked my parents.

After a week of struggling, my parents agreed to help. Charles and Agnes sold their house and moved into my parents' house with their daughter and lived there for three years.

When I was growing up, most Chinese people spent their money very carefully; they usually saved a lot more money then they spent. My parents lived during some of these very difficult times when they were in China. There was no food, which was one of the reasons that they left me with my grandparents. It was very unusual that my parents decided to help my sister and her husband to buy something that they could not afford. My husband and I did not agree about buying something that could not be afforded. We talked to my parents about it, and asked them to think about it very carefully.

My parents complained to me about how difficult it was for them to make such a big decision. They stated that they could not sleep well for a week, but they would not listen to my husband and me.

"They like this land. It was Charles' dream to own a place like this since he was a little boy," my mother repeatedly said to me.

My parents did not have any problems asking my sister for help, but they would not ask me. They complained that I did not help them when they needed help, but they never told me that they needed help when we were on the phone. They felt comfortable asking help from my sister, but not from me.

Charles and Agnes helped my parents do many things. It made my parents feel that they were the only one who helped them. They gave Agnes their own car after she damaged hers in an accident. When Agnes' daughter was born, they opened a bank account for her college education. They told me that they would do the same thing for me after my children were born. My parents never mentioned their promise to me after my daughters were born.

After all this happened, I knew that I could not depend on them at all. I told Curt that we probably would be on our own. Curt was the only child in his family, but he was not spoiled. My in-laws raised him very well. He was very independent and did not ask for anything. I knew everything would be OK for me. God had helped me before, and I trusted that He would help me again.

My father went to China several times by himself. My mother went with him during his last trip. On this trip, they were warmly welcomed by their family and friends. They met with a lot of relatives from my father's family. Everyone took turns inviting my parents for dinner. The food was very delicious but very greasy. My father enjoyed it very much.

My father always enjoyed good food since my sister and I were kids. They did not spend money on fancy clothing or other things, but they would spend money on food. My father believed good health was most important of all. When I was little, each household could only get one pound of pork per person each month. The vegetables in the supermarket were small, dried, and half of them were inedible. My father would pay extra money to buy chicken, fish, fresh vegetables, and fresh fruit from the farmers. The vegetables were picked from the farm in the morning every day and brought to market. We also raised chickens for meat and eggs, because the eggs were very expensive; people gave the eggs as a gift when they visited each other.

After my parents came back from China, my father became very picky about food. He complained that the fish fillets from the supermarket had no flavor. He wanted to buy the whole fish which came with the head and tail, and he wanted to buy ducks, too. He wanted the food that tasted like the food he had in China. My mother did not agree, so they started to argue.

Two years later, my father's health was in trouble. He had high blood pressure, high cholesterol, diabetes, and kidney problems. But it did not stop him from enjoying foods that he liked. He became slower and slower when he was doing things. Sometimes he fell and he could not get up by himself.

He wanted my mother to take him to the Chinese grocery store. In the store, he yelled at my mother because he wanted to buy a duck, and my mother refused. So he bought a duck anyway, and my mother refused to cook it. My father did it by himself and made a mess all over the kitchen.

My mother complained to me when we went to visit. When we were there, she told me that medicine was getting more and more expensive. My father was still getting weaker. One time when my mother was out, he went out to get the mail, and fell on the ground and laid there for one hour. Eventually one of the neighbors found him, and helped him home.

My mother was bitter. She did a lot of things for my father since he was sick, but my father did not appreciate them. He still argued with my mother if things did not go his way. He still wanted to eat greasy food, and he would get angry at my mother if she refused to eat the food that he cooked.

I suggested to my mother that she let my father eat anything that he wanted to eat. I explained to her that not everyone wanted to live a long life by eating vegetables every day. Even Uncle Frank tried to persuade her to let my father eat anything that he wanted. Maybe my father just wanted to enjoy good food for the rest of his life. But my mother refused. The food that she cooked for my father had no oil or salt in it. My father was under my mother's control until the last day of his life.

My mother was stuck in the house. She could not go anywhere, nor could she visit my grandfather who had moved to New Orleans a few years ago. She did not get a last chance to see him before he died.

Agnes and Charles were building their new house. Meanwhile they moved out of my parents' house, and bought a smaller house for themselves. Charles was busy almost all the time. He was an architect and loved to do carpentry. He designed his future home by himself, and liked to do a lot of the jobs himself. Since they bought this land, Charles put all his attention and time into it. When we went to visit, he could not meet with us until dinner time. Sometimes, even then he was absent. He was always doing things on his land, and did not have much time for his family. It made my mother very disappointed.

There were four rooms in this new house. Two were upstairs. They were for my sister, her husband, and their daughter. There were two rooms downstairs, which were for each of my parents. My parents were going to move in after the house was finished, but I did not know this until later. My parents stopped telling me things since I had refused to tell them about Curt's salary. There were many family discussions between my parents, my sister, and her husband. Curt and I were not included until all the decisions were made, and then my mother would tell us when we visited.

"By the way, we decided to do this. Just to let you know."

I had a feeling that the gap between us was growing larger and larger as time passed by, unless I obeyed them for anything and everything. My parents had kept me separated from them since I was born so the gap could never close.

"When are you going to finish building this house? I am afraid there is not much time left for me. I would not be able to see it if it is finished too late," my father said to my sister one time.

His health condition was getting worse and worse. Most of the time, he would not say anything or answer any questions. He sat in the wheelchair, and dropped his head down on to his chest. He had lost most of his energy.

One day, after we arrived at my mother's house, my father pushed his wife. "Go ahead, tell them. Tell them right now," he said with his weak voice. From my experience, I knew that my parents had made a very important decision.

"your father and I decided that we are going to move into your sister's new house as soon as it is finished. We are putting our house on the market to sell now. All the money that we get from selling this house is going to go to your sister. But do not worry; it is just talk right now. Nothing has happened yet," my mother told me.

"OK, if it is your final decision," I said to her calmly. I had already mentally prepared myself that it was going to end this way since the time that they had decided to help Agnes to purchase the land many years ago. It was proven correct on this day.

It meant that from now on, I had to go to Agnes' house every time when we went to visit; this was the house that she bought with her parents' money.

"Have you ever helped us?" All of a sudden, I heard a loud and strong voice from my father, who had been so sick, so weak, and had no energy most of the time. He was attacking me for one last time. He never mentioned all the good things I did for this family in the early years, but he never forgot that I could not help him after they moved so far away from me. He could not forgive me for this, even though he had not asked for help, nor told me that he even needed help.

This was the final nail in the coffin. My father attacked me until the end of his life, and I knew that my mother would do the same. I came to the conclusion that there was no way that they were ever going to examine themselves; they were never going to admit that they were the part of the problem in our relationship. They were too proud to do so, and I could no longer deal with the stress of it.

Everyone is responsible for their own behavior. After my father died, I started to think more often on the things that had happened earlier in my life. I did not want to be any longer with people who did not appreciate me. As a mother, I realized that I needed to live my life for God, for myself, and for my own family. I learned so much from my experiences by watching other people doing things and how they made their decisions. I also learned why some people succeeded in their life and others did not. This life of mine is the one that God arranged for me; it was not by my parents' decision, nor was it by anyone else's.

My previous pastor's wife had said to me one day "you can not choose your parents, but you can choose your own future."